INDEX ON CENSORSHIP 1 2000

WEBSITE NEWS UPDATED WEEKLY

www.indexoncensorship.org
contact@indexoncensorship.org
tel: 020 7278 2313
fax: 020 7278 1878

Volume 29 No 1 January/February 2000 Issue 192

Index on Censorship (ISSN 0306-4220) is published bi-monthly by a non-profit-making company: Writers & Scholars International Ltd, Lancaster House, 33 Islington High Street, London N1 9LH. *Index on Censorship* is associated with Writers & Scholars Educational Trust, registered charity number 325003 *Periodicals postage*: (US subscribers only) paid at Newark, New Jersey. Postmaster: send US address changes to *Index on Censorship* c/o Mercury Airfreight International Ltd Inc, 365 Blair Road, Avenel, NJ 07001, USA
© This selection Writers & Scholars International Ltd, London 1999
© Contributors to this issue, except where otherwise indicated

Subscriptions (6 issues per annum)
Individuals: UK £39, US $52, rest of world £45
Institutions: UK £44, US $80, rest of world £50
Speak to Tony Callaghan on 020 7278 2313

EDITORIAL

Everywhere in chains

It took western media 10 years from the first substantiated report in 1986 to reveal that chattel slavery was still going on in south-western Sudan (p60). No doubt it was because we believe, want to believe, that slavery is dead. In fact, there are approximately 27 million people around the world whose lives are completely controlled by others, and who are paid nothing. As Kevin Bales reports, slavery is alive and well, and 'the key these days is not ownership, but control through violence' (p36). The new slavery is cheap – slaves don't cost much nowadays – but highly profitable. Despite over 300 international treaties and UN conventions signed by most countries of the world, the plight of bonded labourers in India, Javanese women imprisoned in domestic slavery in Saudi Arabia, charcoal burners enslaved in Brazil makes very little impact on a worldwhere human rights are, in theory, high on the agenda.

One new version of slavery is the kidnapping or tricking of women from Eastern Europe into brothels in the West. Offered a new life with job prospects, they find themselves instead inescapably trapped into a life of prostitution. This issue of *Index* addresses other kinds of entrapment too. In Colombia, where fear eats the soul and only the bravest speak out, a disaffected soldier tells a journalist how he has been taught to torture, how massacres are planned, how innocent people are killed to deliver a body count required for promotion (p156). In August this year the famous Colombian comedian, journalist and peace mediator Jaime Garzón (p134) was assassinated, and since then five more journalists have been killed and 11 kidnapped. Our file describes the condition of a country where government, guerrillas and paramilitaries all play their part in a long standing culture of violence.

Malcolm Deas (p116) compares the conflict in Colombia with that in Northern Ireland. The UK's Prevention of Terrorism Act (p84) was an attempt to deal with the Northern Ireland situation – it defines terrorism as the use of violence against the public for political ends. In a new bill just published by the Home Secretary that definition has broadened to cover the *threat* of violence against the public or even against property. The bill also creates a completely new crime in Britain – that of seeking to topple foreign regimes. Where does that leave, for instance, dissident Iraqis opposed to Saddam Hussein's regime? There is a real risk that dissent will be criminalised, that political speech will be regulated, if this bill passes into law. ❏

contents

The slave won't go away. *Index* looks at the contribution that slavery still makes to our lives

Colombia is where the ancient feud between left and right intersects with the monetarised violence of a cocaine-based political economy

LETTERS

The oxygen of publicity
From Mike Bingham, Falkland Islands

I must thank *Index on Censorship* for exposing the harassment I suffered as a result of my research in the Falkland Islands (Enemy of the People, *Index* 5/1999). Since your article appeared I have received dozens of letters supporting my fight to protect penguins, and the campaign against me has stopped.

The story was virtually censored in the Falklands. The government-funded newspaper was sent copies of *Index*, the *Sunday Times*, *Observer* and *Guardian* but made no mention of the report. The Falklands radio station (also government-funded) dismissed the story, describing it as 'sensationalised'. They read out a Falklands government denial, which was so untruthful I asked for the right to reply. The radio station refused.

The authorities did, however, clean up their act. An MP raised the matter in parliament and the British government sent a police and criminal justice adviser over. I received an apology and an admission that a false document was used to arrest me and another person's criminal convictions used in a second attempt to arrest me.

Falklands Conservation denied harassment, but admitted that they dismissed me because 'there was concern about the level of publicity oiled birds were getting'. Their conservation officer has resigned and left the Falklands.

The publicity from your article has allowed justice to flourish briefly in the Falklands.

Falklands fight back
From Sukey Cameron, Falkland Islands Government UK Representative

Michael Griffin's article raises important issues. The Falkland Islands government takes environmental issues seriously, spending over £5 million a year on fisheries research and protection and, prior to oil-licensing it established an environmental forum.

When Mr Bingham's contract with Falklands Conservation ended he was employed by the government, working at Stanley Power Station (the reference to 'the local power company' is misleading).

Mr Bingham already has a resident's permit and applied for a permanent resident's permit. The handling of his applications has been complicated by various legal difficulties. This has not operated to his disadvantage.

The Royal Falkland Islands Police found no evidence of a break-in at his property. Mr Bingham pleaded guilty on two counts of importing prohibited goods and procuring an obscene article through the post. It is regrettable that confusion arose over the question of previous offences. Information from the National Criminal Intelligence Services contained nothing which indicated it concerned a different man.

Mr Bingham clearly has not had a happy time in the Falklands. But the Falkland Islands government is not involved in, and has not promoted, any campaign to intimidate or hound him, or deprive him of his rights.

First count your penguins
From Ann Brown, UK Secretary, Falklands Conservation

We wish to correct a number of statements which question the integrity of our organisation. The figures quoted on the Falklands penguin population are misleading. A 1932 count found 3 million pairs. There have been three major declines in the population since then. Falklands Conservation has undertaken intensive studies of this for the last 14 years. There is no known single reason for the declines and no significant scientific evidence to link them with squid fishing.

The figures you quote as Mr Bingham's are from our penguin census. Figures in the *Atlas of Breeding Birds of the Falkland Islands* were compiled 12 years before the census and are not 'rival' figures.

An oil rig arrived in April 1998 (not 1997). Oil from oiled birds was analysed as 'heavy crude' and is not attributable to exploratory drilling.

Michael Bingham was employed on a three-year contract. When it expired it was extended for 12 months. He applied for further work with us, but was not successful. He had made a false claim on his original application.

Our organisation did not change in 1996 because of the appointment of 'councillors and directors involved in oil, fishing and shipping'. Two new Falkland Island trustees were appointed that year: neither was an island councillor.

Falklands Conservation is an independent NGO and a UK registered charity. Our government grant amounted to 32% of our total income in 1997/98. There is no 'cosy arrangement' with the government: protection of wildlife is our sole objective. ❑

● **Fancy that!** Four days after being accepted as an official candidate for membership of the European Union, Turkey said it will ease restrictions on use of the Kurdish language. 'Everyone living in Turkey,' said Foreign Minister Ismail Cem, 'should have the right to broadcast in their own language.'

● **Le Web** From the province that brought the Oeuf McMuffin and McPoulet comes news that Louise Beaudoin, the Quebec 'language minister', is now insisting that commercial websites aimed at people living in the province must be available in French. Nintendo and Sony had until New Year's Eve to comply, or be fined.

● **Ugly rumours** Cambodia's government is to sue the aptly-named *Kate Cheat Khmer* newspaper over a 'highly irresponsible' report that condoms on sale had been manufactured in Vietnam and deliberately tainted with HIV to induce AIDS. Cambodia was occupied by Vietnam for 10 years after the 1979 invasion which ousted the Khmer Rouge regime.

● **Dung as art...** Belarusian painter Alek Pushkin was arrested on 11 November for dumping a wheelbarrow of manure along with President Alyksandr Lukashenka's portrait, state symbols and local banknotes outside the presidential office. He argued that the act was an artistic performance intended to 'say thank you' for the president's time in office. He requested that an expert art evaluation be included in his trial for 'malicious hooliganism and profaning state symbols'.

● **Dung as blasphemy** Feigning illness to lull a security guard, Dennis Heiner, 72, ducked behind a plexiglass shield at the Brooklyn Museum of Art to squeeze white paint over the face and body of *The Holy Virgin Mary*, by British artist Chris Ofili. The painting, decorated with elephant dung, was part of the Sensation exhibition, which incurred the wrath of New York's Mayor Rudolph Giuliani (*Index* 6/1999). When the guard asked why he had done it, Heiner replied: 'It's blasphemous.'

● **Boppathon for burial** The last earthly possessions of the 39 members of the Heaven's Gate cult, who committed mass suicide nearly three years ago, have been auctioned to cover their burial costs. Entrepreneurs snapped up clothes, cookbooks, metal-frame beds, a sewing machine and a collection of books about UFOs to sell on the Internet, or display in a Museum of Death, due to open in Hollywood in January. The cult believed that, by killing themselves, they would come back to life on a spaceship flying in the wake of the Hale-Bopp comet.

● **Bunker in the sky** Inter-service rivalry was suspected when Russia's Space Agency stole a march on the Strategic Rocket Force (SRF) by announcing in November that all its systems – including those on the Mir space station – were Y2K compliant. As for Russia's missiles, all the secretive SRF would concede was that de-bugging was 'nearing completion'. Readers who fled to Mir over the new year in the expectation of nuclear catastrophe may wish to decamp promptly as, millennium compliant or not, Mir is expected to enter the earth's atmosphere and burn up in March.

● **Is that a camera in your pocket, or...?** As the clock struck 12 on millenium night, a new law passed onto California's statute books outlawing covert photography up a woman's skirt 'with intent to arouse, appeal to or gratify the lust, passions or sexual desires'. The legislation came about following the Disneyland arrest of a man caught videoing women with a camera concealed in a dufflebag. The bemused district attorney found himself unable to prosecute under any existing law. Naturally, blame for the rash of 'upskirt' peepers has been placed squarely on the Internet where a host of like-minded websites are claimed to encourage all manner of inventive voyeuristic schemes.

● **Triple whammy** Israel built up for the millennium with tidal waves of scandal. After the national team's 8-0 thrashing by Denmark, a journalist revealed that some team members had spent the night before the match with call girls. Five players started an Internet site to fight against the 'witch-hunt'. Meanwhile, Ofer Nimrodi, millionaire publisher of *Ma'ariv* newspaper, was detained over allegations he had paid hit-men to assassinate a witness in his trial for wire-tapping. Israeli TV broadcast a clip of Nimrodi in a police cell, tearing off a strip of paper from a document, putting it in his mouth and swallowing it. A third scandal involves former prime minister Benjamin Netanyahu who is being interrogated over bribery allegations. One involves building contractor Avner Amedi's claim that he provided the Netanyahus with over US$100,000 worth of services. If 'Bibi' is found guilty, he could quickly pay off the debts through his US$50,000 lectures. His preferred subject? 'Leadership and Integrity'.

● **Flirting with *fatwa*** Award-winning documentary maker, Rob Gardner, is to film a history of Islam with the active approval, support and co-operation of his hosts – the Iranian government. The authorities apparently took Gardner's word that he would present a 'positive view of Islam', offering a permit without so much as asking to see the script. The initial reaction in the US was to reject the venture because of economic sanctions imposed following the 1979 occupation of the US Embassy in Tehran. An exemption was finally found through the help of sympathetic senators.

● **Turning in his grave** The 14 October raid by NATO on a Bosnian Croatian spying centre in the divided city of Mostar has opened a can of worms that the late President Franjo Tudjman would be only too glad to avoid – wherever he is now. A multinational force of 1,500 NATO troops captured 42 computers, 10,000 documents and truckloads of spying equipment from four buildings. A senior NATO official said the raid had uncovered 'prima facie evidence of linkages' between the Croatian government and local intelligence officials that were specifically designed to undermine the Dayton Accords of 1995. Tudjman, who died in early December, funneled millions of dollars a month into the spy network. In turn, it sought to recruit 'loyal' agents among the local staffs of the UN, Red Cross, NATO, the office of the International High Representative in Bosnia and the UN War Crimes Tribunal at The Hague itself.

● **Dear Reggie** A whiff of fakery emanates from the copy of a letter written in the dark days of 1943 from our man in Moscow, Ambassador Sir Archibald Clerk Kerr, to Lord Pembroke at the Foreign Office. Our source claims it was released under the 30-year rule; the document is nearly twice that age, but we publish it here because of its balanced prose style – and the contribution it may one day make to the expanding field of war mythology. 'My Dear Reggie,' writes Sir Archie, 'In these dark days man tends to look for little shafts of light that spill from Heaven. My days are probably darker than yours and I need, my God I do, all the light I can get. But I am a decent fellow and I do not want to be mean and selfish about what little brightness is shed upon me from time to time. So I propose to share with you a tiny flash that has illuminated my sombre life and tell you that God has given me a new Turkish colleague whose card tells me that he is called Mustapha Kunt. We all feel like that Reggie, especially when Spring is upon us, but few of us would care to put it on our cards. It takes a Turk to do that.'

● **Execution by stealth** Japan is not particularly proud that it retains the death penalty, though a recent survey found that four out of five citizens support capital punishment. So when the judiciary finally implements its dread decisions, it makes sure they happen as quietly as snow dropping into water. It was only last year that the Justice Ministry actually acknowledged that hangings took place at all.

Since 1993, the Christmas season has also become the hanging season with a clutch of executions rushed through between the parliamentary recess and the holidays to avoid undue attention. Last year was no exception. On 16 December Teruo Ono, 62, was led out of Fukuoka Detention House in Tokyo and hanged, having spent 21 years on death row for the rape, murder and robbery of a woman in 1977. What was particularly shocking was that he had applied for a re-trial, claiming there had been irregularities in the court documents of two previous appeals. Kazuo Sagawa, executed on the same day, had been on death row for 18 years. His lawyers had filed a 'request for protection' from the court against the prison authorities which dispatched him.

Neither hanging caused much stir in the Japanese press, although the first Ono would have heard of his approaching death would have been moments before he was led to the scaffold. Executions are carried out without the knowledge of families or lawyers and prisoners are held for years in solitary with little opportunity for contact with anyone except prison guards.

A recent case which illustrated the cruelty of life on death row was that of Ota Katsunori, who was found dead in Sapporo Detention Centre on 8 November. After 15 years inside, he committed suicide by slashing his throat with a razor blade while taking a bath. He wrote three suicide notes.

Michael Griffin

● **For unknown reasons** In 1999 some 20 journalists in Ethiopia were arrested under the 1993 Press Law, many without trial or formal charges. Journalists reporting in politically sensitive areas, notably Oromo, the Somali regions and the capital, Addis Ababa, were especially vulnerable. Private press and radio stations bore the brunt, particularly the independent *Urigi* and *Tobia* newspapers. *Urigi*, an Amharic language title owned by an Oromo company, is suspected by the government of collaborating with the Oromo Liberation Front (OLF).

Urigi has published stories on illegal detentions, torture, disappearance and extrajudicial execution throughout the subdued but consistent conflict between the government of President Meles Zenawi government and the OLF in Oromo. In September 1997 general manager Garuma Bekel was detained after publishing an article which likened prison conditions in the Black Lion Hospital in Addis to a 'Nazi concentration camp'. *Urigi*'s deputy editor Tesfaye Deressa was arrested one month later, as was acting editor Solomon Namara, in connection with an article alleging that the shooting by police of three Oromos in Addis' Mekanissa area was tantamount to an extrajudicial execution. Nine days later Bekel was re-arrested depite the fact he had left the newspaper to join a new Oromo human rights organisation. The *Urigi* journalists remain imprisoned on charges of 'inciting terrorist activity' and 'defamation of news'.

This catalogue of harassment is echoed at the privately-run *Tobia*, which has suffered from the most arrests and suspensions of any Ethiopian newspaper to date. Up to 10 journalists and administrative staff were detained in January 1998, hours after the paper's offices were burned down. *Tobia*'s problems arise largely from its editorial opposition to government policy, but also from reflecting the prevaling pessimism of the country.

Other journalists have been imprisoned 'for unknown statements', a chilling phrase. Tamerat Gemeda of *Seyle Nebelbal* has been in prison in Mekali prison since 4 June in Addis Ababa 'for unknown reasons'. Zemedkun Moges of Atkourot was imprisoned in March 1997 but details of the arrest have still to be made public. Bezunesh Debebe, publisher and and deputy editor of the Amharic weekly *Zegabi*, has been detained since 10 June.

Shifa Rahman

● **The beast lives** Readers of all good news outlets, from the *New York Times* to *PC Magazine,* might have thought that the US government's anti-trust action against Microsoft concluded in November with Judge Thomas Jackson heaving a judicial brick through Bill Gates' ubiquitous Windows. In fact, instead of blasting Windows' domination of the operating system market, the judge ruled that Microsoft's crime was the use of that monopoly to smother competitors of the company's other products.

Manufacturers who dared to put Netscape's Navigator icon on the Windows desktop were informed that, 'Mr Gates was *really mad*' and might just rip Windows out of their machines. Instead of crimes against computing humanity, the judge named only a short list of victims who are themselves niche monopolists – AOL (owners of Netscape), Sun Microsystems, Intel. The findings reduced the overhyped battle to a squabble between elites over desktop turf.

Judge Jackson, by giving the Windows monopoly his grudging blessing, eliminates any threat that in the next phase of the trial he will pry open the core monopoly to competitors like Linux. For the court's mercy, Gates owes thanks to Joel Klein, head of the US Justice Department Anti-Trust Division. Klein confirmed his backdown when we spoke in August. 'The acquisition of the Windows monopoly we do not challenge,' he said, reversing the entire thrust of his original case. He knew that eliminating the comforting uniformity of the Windows monopoly would create havoc for PC users. He misquoted Rex Harrison: 'I've grown accustomed to its face.'

Nevertheless, the judge gave enough ammo to AOL, Sun and IBM to bring separate claims under US anti-trust compensation laws. Of course, we can imagine a sly Gates even now settling the whole shooting match with a flimflam reorganisation. Anti-trust experts have proposed creating several 'baby bills', each licenced to sell Windows in competition with each other. Gates won't go for that, but we can expect him to propose spinning off the Web Browser and Applications Divisions from the Windows business, each carefully preserving their unique monopoly.

Legally, Microsoft is home safe, but the fairy tale of Gates the Entrepreneur is nailed. Over 207 pages, Judge Jackson detailed Microsoft's widening dominance in computing by means of vicious, illegal, bully-boy tactics, from coercion to sabotage. Gates did not capture the market by inventing the better mousetrap, but by turning into the nastiest rat in the sewer to the future. ❏

Greg Palast

We apologise for printing the wrong title for John le Carré's latest book in our last issue *(Index 6/1999)*. The book is called *Single & Single* (Hodder and Stoughton, 1999)

CHRISTIAN CARYL

Objectivity to order

Access is the key problem for journalists reporting on the second Chechen war, and is under tight military control

A few months ago I attended a Moscow conference that brought together journalists and policymakers from Russia and the West. At one point a young Russian, a deputy in a provincial parliament, asked the assembled foreigners: 'During the Kosovo crisis we all saw how western media whipped up public sentiment in the NATO countries in favour of military action against the Serbs. There are many people here in Russia today who say that we lack some way of mobilising society in a similar way. So could you please explain to us how you managed to do that?'

It was a question that senior Russian politicians have been asking themselves. On 7 October, shortly after the beginning of what is now being called the second Chechen war, Prime Minister Vladimir Putin oversaw the creation of a new government organisation called the Russian Information Centre, or Rosinformtsentr. The centre represents a realisation among the political elite that neither brute censorship nor complete permissiveness will serve government interests. Most of the Rosinformtsentr staffers are journalists from the government-run RIA Novosti News Agency. The director, Mikhail Margelov, is a journalist and public relations professional who, by his own admission, belonged for a while to the old Soviet KGB. As a sign of his team's relative savvy, one of their first innovations was the creation of their own website *www.infocentre.ru*, designed in part to compete with two Chechen sites *www.kavkaz.org* and *www.amina.com*, widely used by western journalists desperate for views from the hard-to-reach rebels.

An article published on 7 October on the opening of the centre in the government's official daily, *Rossiiskaya Gazeta*, stated: 'It is to be hoped that the Rosinformtsentr will learn the lessons of past Chechen events, when the country and the world effectively divided into two camps.' According to conventional wisdom in Moscow, one of the reasons for the Russian army's catastrophic defeat in the 1994–96 war was its failure to develop a coherent press policy. Both Russian and foreign journalists ranged about the lines with relative freedom, and produced dramatic evidence of the Russian forces' general disarray.

Now the new press minister, Mikhail Lesin, has publicly criticised leading military officers for not being open with the media, arguing that they should provide journalists with better access to the war zone. This echoes the views of western journalists who feel that the real problem lies with the military, which still tends to shut journalists off rather than considering the benefits of managed co-operation with them.

Access has remained tightly controlled, however, and Rosinformtsentr's guided tours into Chechnya have scarcely been triumphs of proactive news management. I travelled to Chechnya with nine Western European colleagues at the beginning of December on a long-pleaded-for trip organised by Rosinformtsentr. The Russian officials accompanying us reiterated that we would have complete freedom within the limits of the itinerary (and subject to security considerations). In practice, of course, things were more ambiguous. At the first stop we were brought to a house said to belong to a Chechen field commander who had kept kidnap victims in a hole in the shed in his backyard – an idea immediately contradicted by a Russian neighbour: 'Nope, there were no hostages here,' he told us cheerfully. 'I would have known.' As other journalists gathered, our Russian minders broke into the conversation, saying that our time was up.

The pattern was repeated throughout the trip. When Chechens had positive things to say about Russian policy (and some of them did), our minders were happy to let them discourse at length. But when a Chechen woman in Chervlennaya began to tell us about high casualties among the civilian population, one of the men accompanying us pushed his way through and began denouncing her as a provocateur. Several TV crews filmed the scene which must have given their viewers a less than flattering image of Russian information policy.

Despite these rather patchy attempts at intimidation, most of us were able to garner a variety of views – some of them extremely critical of Moscow. At a lunch hosted by Russian military officials, a press spokesman for the Russian forces in Chechnya lectured us, Soviet-style, on the need for 'objectivity and truth' in our reporting. 'If you don't write objectively,' he said, 'we won't let you come back again.' Interestingly, one of our Rosinformtsentr minders winced at this heavy-handedness – another indication of the divide between civilian would-be news managers and their less sophisticated military counterparts.

Few journalists, and very few foreign ones, have been able to get into the war zone. On the side of the Chechen rebels, widespread kidnappings and, in some cases, executions of foreign hostages have added to the risks that journalists face. Meanwhile, Russian officialdom has kept extremely tight control over travel. After my return from Chechnya, a Rosinformtsentr official told me that there were 200 news organisations from around the world on the waiting list for trips into the Russian-controlled zone.

By and large, the Russian media have done their best to follow the advice given by Defence Minister Igor Sergeev at the Rosinformtsentr inauguration: 'He believes the actions of Russian soldiers and officers should be covered to reflect the present-day momentum so as to make them feel "needed by society" and to boost their morale, ORT TV reported on 7 October.

The fact that censorship has been primarily self-imposed became apparent on 5 December, when the private NTV news channel used a high-profile news programme to show several segments on the war that called into question the official version of events. One even quoted military experts who suggested that the death toll among Russian soldiers was much higher than officially acknowledged. Meanwhile, the scrappy independent newspaper *Novaya Gazeta* has been highly critical of the war.

But *Novaya Gazeta*'s circulation is small, and it is television, not the papers, that moulds public opinion in Russia. The sad fact is that censorship is scarcely required when most media empires are either financially ailing, tightly subordinated to their owners' political agendas, or both. Under such circumstances a threat of intensified financial pressure from the government (via the tax authorities) is usually enough to bring media managers into line. But there is also the fact that Putin's waging of the war remains popular with the public. And until that changes, coverage of the war by the Russian media is unlikely to change either. ❏

Christian Caryl *is the Moscow Bureau Chief of* US News and World Report *magazine. He has spent the past 15 years in central and eastern Europe and has written for the* Spectator, *the* New Republic *and the* Wall Street Journal

ALEXSEY SIMONOV

Knock from below

Russia's brutal assault on Chechnya has revealed more than the political value of a distant war – it has also exposed the crisis facing Russian journalism

It was ever thus: the authorities, military authorities in particular, seek to suppress information or release it in a doctored form, and journalists try to uncover it. Clearly the most effective way of preventing the release of undesirable facts or the emergence of another point of view is to turn reporters away. For maximum effect you can arrange a cover-up and spoon-feed journalists with whatever information you please.

As we have seen, the Russian authorities have achieved this pretty successfully up till now. During the first Chechen war, their state of confusion gave journalists the chance to uncover the real stories and, up to a point, resist official mendacity. It is difficult to wage war without ideological back-up and, at that time, the military lacked any kind of intellectual underpinning. Attempts to reinstate ideological clichés going back to WWII, which had shaped reporting on the war in Afghanistan, were no longer effective and the strongmen weren't up to much more.

The first Chechen war saw the media defending the principle of objective information. They still found it rebarbative, then, to lie and listen to others lying to them. But it seems to me now that many of those who did magnificent work during that war have grown so weary that even this principle has become a source of indifference to them. That is the reason why they are producing nothing but rhetoric about 'the enemy' and 'strikes on the enemy' all the more since the September bomb attacks in Moscow have finally given shape to the nebulous image of our opponent.

The facts have become compartmentalised in the usual way: 'the enemy', 'the people', 'the collective'... And that is what the strongmen are striving for – to turn public interest away from real human beings and the problems they now face. In these circumstances, it is quite natural that journalists have nothing to say when the man in uniform announces on television that 'refugees attempted to break through the border'. The language activates a stereotype. To 'break through the border' is a bad thing. One is reminded of the heroic WWII border-guard Karatsupa and his wise dog, whose exploits have since slipped into the language.

But the predicate obscures the subject. The refugees who 'broke through' the border were women and children. And, in addition, a new stereotype – 'the Chechen border' – is superimposed on the old. In the past it was always said that there *is* no border. Chechnya is a part of the Russian Federation; this is the restoration of the constitutional order... And now it turns out that the border for which Chechens fought does indeed exist. Illegal border crossings can happen. Even if the transgressor is an infant, stereotypes prevail. And then we hear the familiar report that 'terrorists are using human shields...' We can't see this happening from where we are, jounalists haven't seen it either; and there is no information available from the other side.

In the first war, the initial victory on the information front went to the Chechen. Nobody from the Russian side conducted a serious analysis of the position and role of the media in the campaign. We did not attempt to make sense of its beginning, its development or the increasing fatigue of the press as it moved towards 'a more balanced interpretation', when abuses committed by the Chechen side also came into view. For me, the Chechen lost their credibility when NTV correspondant Lena Masyuk was taken hostage in 1997 and the authorities showed they were unable to free her or keep to what they themselves have called Caucasian norms of civilised behaviour.

Journalists effectively lost their chance to work in Chechnya. The loss of information which the Chechen side now has to endure is linked to its own behaviour.

When *Izvestiya's* Valery Yakov went to Pervomaiskoye in 1995 to research his report, he knew that the ordinary Chechens would help him. Today either the story would be doomed, or he himself. And it is doubtless no coincidence that we at the Glasnost Defence Foundation failed to produce a book about the end of the war, even through we were very keen to show how the collapse of public information occurred. Where the information war is concerned, the recent explosions in Moscow were not just outrageous on the part of the Chechen (if they were indeed responsible) but also very foolish.

On the other hand, Russian journalists still haven't learnt to talk tough. During the last war, interviews with field commanders were evidently 'packaged', and the package was a Chechen one. Journalists spoke with Chechen commanders a lot less freely than with Russian generals. This is also true today. There have been discussions on whether the Chechen military commander Khattab should be shown on television. What is more to the point is that apparently Khattab can be shown only if he wants to be shown, and it would be impossible to imagine a correspondant telling him directly what he thinks of him. And if, for example, the former vice-premier and warlord Shamil Basayev were to decide that he wanted to speak with a Russian correspondent, the interview should take place only on condition that he is forced to answer impartial questions. He should say not what he wants to say, but what is likely to be of interest to viewers or readers. And the decision to use the interview should be based solely on that.

And how is it that Khattab, apparently a Jordanian by origin, speaks Russian so well? Where did he learn? Perhaps he was taught in one of those central Asian training camps for terrorists and a present general of ours was his tutor. No one is investigating this...

We know intuitively that we are being lied to. But what are these lies? That is something we can no longer tell. When we hear of the astonishing accuracy of the bombing, this begs questions. What has happened – have they been doing extra training? Has more petrol and kerosene suddenly become available? Are they using improved weapons? We don't know. Previous experience suggests that this is rubbish. And then we hear in passing that the Dagestani volunteers have died as a result of inaccurate artillery – fire and aviation. But who is now in any position to compare the triumphalist accounts of the strongmen with a brief flash of honest journalism? Who could possibly gather the mass of crucial information that counter the official line? And how?

Our present pseudo-ideology is descending the slippery slope of 'national-patriotism'. Our prime ministers – Primakov, Stepanshin, Putin – are all representatives of government security departments, which indicates that this ideology of ersatz-patriotism will continue to predominate. It will also dominate the consciousness of journalists themselves. Specially fomented hysteria allows us to forget the details and facts. We were informed of the discovery of rebel strongholds in Dagestani villages. We were promised an investigation. How could these fighters have spent two and a half years building up bases in Dagestan? And what? Nothing. In *Novaya Gazeta*, Yuri Shchekochikhin has written that he seen none of these reported strongholds in Dagestani villages and that the military are lying. But no conclusions have been drawn from this. His report slipped through the net, as though it had never been.

In *Moskovskiye Novosti* Alexander Zhilin wrote that militiamen and soldiers, including conscripts in their first year of military service, are being taken to Dagestan from all over Russia. At the same time, 80,000 Armenian soldiers and officers and 90,000 internal troops have filtered into the northern Caucasian military zone, a total of 170,000. According to information released by the military, the number of Chechen fighters was never more than 2,000. Are we to conclude that they have 2,000 Suvorovs [a nineteenth-century officer]? That they fight not with numbers but with skill? And what about us? I want to know why and I have no means of finding out. They don't answer questions like that. They say it's unpatriotic to ask … 'military secrets', 'strategy'… But in Russia things are never investigated after the event. If we don't clarify them now, we never will.

The dream of the security services and the strongmen is being well and truly realised. Journalists have been turned away from the action. With rare exceptions, they are taking information directly from the authorities. No consolidation of the information space, no broadening of the capacity to acquire information is having any influence on the situation. What's more, attempts are being made in the regions to close down the few information channels that are slightly out of step.

And the journalists appear to be weary of one another. When we proposed that state-owned NTV should interview the nuclear whistle-blower Grigory Pasko, who had just arrived in Moscow, they explained that his story was no longer 'new'. No hard feelings. We've had enough, that's all. How much of one thing can you take...? The same is happening with this war, and the quality of journalism has dropped.

While I was defending journalists' rights on behalf of the Glasnost Defence Foundation, I felt that, at the very least, I understood what I was doing. But in all honesty I now no longer know who I should be defending, and from whom. In our book *The Information War in Chechnya* (Glasnost Defence Foundation, 1997), we exposed the falsification to which we were being subjected. But now we have nothing to draw on. We don't know where the truth lies. Four years ago people came to us proposing joint projects: this time there has been not a single attempt to use the Foundation as a public platform or in any other way.

I don't know how things will end with Chechnya and Dagestan and I shall not attempt to make any predictions. I'm certain, though, that the state of the press will continue to deteriorate until the presidential elections. It will reach its nadir around election time. After that there are two possible alternatives: either it will turn out that there is yet further to fall (I am reminded of Stanislav Lec's image: 'I sank into the depths; and heard a knock from below') or, with immense difficulty, we shall begin to recover our professional pride and self-sufficiency. But there can hardly be a worse time for self-examination than during an election against the backcloth of war. ❏

Alexsey Simonov is executive director of the Glasnost Defence Foundation in Moscow. Translated by Irena Maryniak

MICHAEL YOUNG

The lid on memory

Ten years after the war, Lebanon still can't answer the question: where do you hide 17,000 corpses?

The tenuous voice on the soundtrack belongs to law professor Emile Sheaib. What he has agreed to impart to film-maker Bahije Hojeij for his documentary film *Makhtufun* (Kidnapped) is more than a story, it is a state of mind. Where the law demands precision, the abduction in 1985 of Sheaib's son, André, brought him not just tremendous suffering, but ambiguity. Sheaib's particular nightmare is to inhabit the disorder of a narrative with no ending.

The narrative has had frequent interruptions. When his son was kidnapped Sheaib became easy prey for extortion. As he puts it, a 'cornucopia of middlemen' approached him offering information on André's supposed whereabouts, in exchange for cash. Caught between a need to find his son – or at least discover what happened to him – and a refusal to let a potentially good lead slide, Sheaib borrowed money and sold his belongings to raise the ransoms. All to no avail. Nothing has been heard from André Sheaib.

Last October, an organisation called the Committee of the Families of the Kidnapped and Disappeared in Lebanon sought to remind the government of the 17,000 or so people who vanished between 1975 and 1990, the long night of Lebanon's wars. The committee, established in West Beirut in 1982, launched a campaign to find common ground with the authorities, who have assiduously avoided investigating the fate of the disappeared.

The pattern of official prevarication was set in the 1980s, when three parliamentary committees were established. Their efforts came to nothing, since the militiamen who arranged the abductions were far more powerful in those days than Lebanon's supine legislators. Yet when the conflict ended, the families of the disappeared discovered that they faced an obstacle more perverse than the chaos of the war years: national amnesia.

Those who inherited power in Lebanon were the most capable of the wartime commanders. Several measures abetted their metamorphoses into pillars of the post-war oligarchy, absolving them of responsibility for their wartime crimes. As a result, even an award-winning documentary such as Hojeij's was too hot to be broadcast on national television – it might have disturbed the postwar serenity decreed by the authorities.

The most notable of the government's self-protection measures came in August 1991, when Omar Karami's government issued a general amnesty pardoning those who had engaged in a variety of wartime crimes, including the fomenting of civil and confessional conflict and politically motivated murder. While most war criminals were exonerated, however, pardon was denied to those who had engaged in bank fraud, the smuggling of antiquities and the selling of property to foreigners without a licence.

The Committee of the Families was incensed. Its members had not spent eight years trying to secure the release of their loved ones only to sanction absolution. When the committee was first established, perhaps as many as a thousand people were abducted by the Israelis and their Lebanese allies. The majority were Muslims and their abductors believed them opposed to the Christian leadership which the Israelis had helped bring to power. This determined the initial religious composition of the committee, which was largely Muslim.

However, the war was ecumenical in its selection of victims. In the mid-1980s a similar grouping was established in predominantly Christian East Beirut to demand the release of individuals caught 'on the other side'. The Muslim-Christian divide appeared not to affect the relatives of the disappeared, who merged into one group at the war's end, in spite of militia attempts to stir up religious animosity between the families at the height of the hostilities.

The families' task changed once the fighting stopped. Rather than attempting to obtain the release of those abducted, the families concentrated on gathering information on their fate. Implicit in this was a recognition that the kidnapped were dead. Many had long accepted this. More problematic are those who continue to presume the contrary. Practically all those in the committee believe their relatives are still alive.

Disappeared, Beirut, Lebanon – Credit: Sallie Shatz

Their hope resides in a sophism that plays on the fact that many of those abducted vanished without a trace: where, they ask, does one hide 17,000 corpses?

Where indeed? And yet the same could be asked of 17,000 living human beings who, one must presume, are languishing in approximately 17,000 cellars and eating up the reserves of their increasingly destitute captors. There is a further paradox in the committee's post-war demands: though most members assumed the disappeared were alive, the committee's representatives sought for several years to persuade the state to declare the missing dead, if a commission of inquiry so determined.

This posed major problems for the authorities. Virtually everything in the new republic makes the appointment of a commission of inquiry improbable. Not only would it embarrass several former warlords who, as elected parliamentarians, would be called upon to approve its establishment, but it would also reopen a Pandora's box of wartime recrimination.

Lebanon's leaders have also been reluctant to approve a measure that is potentially harmful to business. After Rafiq al-Hariri became prime minister in 1992 there was a concerted effort to put a lid on memory. Hariri sought to introduce a new social order, the central tenet of which was that Lebanon had jettisoned all its wartime enmities. Hariri's society was to be inherently harmonious, united by a desire to make money and entice foreign investors to Beirut. The imbroglio of the disappeared was an impediment to both the political order which sustained Hariri and the vision he was trying to peddle. His successors have stayed on course.

The committee's demand for a collective declaration of death raised a host of legal problems, particularly with the Muslim judicial hierarchy. The Muslim courts have authority over personal status issues, including inheritance, and such a declaration would have bypassed them. The authorities' misgivings were compounded by the fact that they deny responsibility for the disappearances: the state, they argue, was absent during the war years.

Hariri thought he had solved the problem in April 1995 when parliament passed a law shortening the period required for families to have abducted relatives legally declared dead. While this was done to speed up inheritance procedures, it was rejected by the families because it forced them to initiate judicial proceedings to effectively 'kill' their loved ones. To add insult to injury, the government ignored the committee's proposals for new legislation on the disappeared.

The episode was preceded by an unusual statement in January 1995 from the parliament speaker, Nabih Birri, himself a one-time militia leader. As parliament prepared to discuss the draft law on the legal declaration of death, Birri bluntly announced that there were no survivors among the disappeared. The statement was revealing in that a public figure could blithely admit that thousands of people had been murdered, without provoking a public backlash.

Retribution is a matter on which the Committee of the Families remains divided. The more pragmatic understand that the authorities will reject their demands, even the obtainable ones, for as long as they believe the families seek retribution. Others, following the example of Chile and Argentina, play on officials' fears by insisting that now is the time to bring former wartime leaders to justice.

That is unlikely, however, and for now the pragmatists prevail. The committee has been so marginalised in recent years that President Emile Lahoud has neglected to meet with its representatives. It was to avoid becoming inconsequential that they reformulated their aims in October, reducing them to three demands which the government might eventually consider.

First, the committee called, once again, for the formation of a commission of inquiry which would publish its findings within a year. Significantly, it did not request a collective declaration of death. The authorities find a commission of inquiry distasteful, but might accept some sort of body which declares that the disappeared have not been found, while avoiding pronouncing them dead.

Second, the committee called on the government to institute a social programme to assist relatives of the disappeared. And finally, it requested that 13 April, regarded as the date of the start of the Lebanese war, be set aside as a 'day for memory and the disappeared'. It called, in addition, for the building of a monument to the victims of war crimes. Both demands may be acceptable to the state, within certain limits, and the symbolic force of a well-designed monument should not be underestimated.

Timorousness is a potent feature of Lebanon's post-war psyche. The authorities are likely to postpone a decision for as long as they can but at some stage, the Committee of the Families calculates, they might become uncomfortable. The families may then be given something to alleviate their burden, though it will certainly fall short of an answer to the question: What happened? ❏

Michael Young *was editor of the quarterly* Lebanon Report*, and writes a weekly political column in Beirut's English-language paper, the* Daily Star

LISA FORRELL

Crossed lines

New UK legislation will undo a centuries-old tradition protecting private individuals against state intrusions

Secreted somewhere in the middle of the Queen's Speech in November, setting out the government's programme, was a reference to proposed legislation extending the scope of telephone tapping and secret surveillance. No sooner had that happened than a large bug in the form of a steel box was discovered concealed in the bodywork of Gerry Adams' Ford Mondeo. When confronted with the possibility that this was the work of the British secret service, a spokesperson for the prime minister said, 'The security and intelligence services operate within the law.'

In a world of complex organised crime and terrorist activity, the need for equally sophisticated methods of detection is understandable. But that must be balanced against the right to privacy of the individual, as enshrined by the European Convention on Human Rights and now incorporated into English law by the Human Rights Act (which comes into force next October). These rights should be treated as inalienable, and only subject to the most precise of restrictions. They are not.

There are four ways the authorities can have your telephone calls intercepted or your post opened without your knowledge. The police may apply for a warrant under the Police Act; MI6 and MI5 may tap your phones under the Intelligence Services Act and the Security Services Act respectively; finally, the secretary of state can issue warrants under the Interception of Communications Act. Theoretically, four different organs of state could be interfering with your privacy at any one time.

These surveillances effectively overturn a centuries–old tradition condemning warrants authorising intrusion into property by a secretary of state in the classic case of *Entick v Carrington* in 1765. Most of this legislation occurred under a Conservative government not known for its overwhelming concern for human rights. Now a Labour government which claims to be committed to constitutional rights has proposed legislation to broaden the scope of interference and cement the previous regime's draconian legislation.

Home Office proposals published last year state that permissible interception should include the breadth of new technology, such as mobile phones, faxes and e-mail. Communication service providers will be compelled to create systems capable of interference (and reasonably assist the authorities when intercepting), all of which will make them less private and secure. In addition, the law will expand to include both public and private networks (such as hotels and workplaces).

The grounds for obtaining interception warrants remain as in the old law. They are: i) interests of national security; ii) preventing or detecting serious crime; or iii) safeguarding the economic well-being of the UK. These criteria are a cause of legitimate concern. National security and economic well-being are not defined and could be subjectively interpreted. When these grounds were first suggested, the then government refused to accept an opposition (Labour) amendment which would have restricted national security warrants to those connected with subversion, terrorism or espionage. Where is that sentiment now? Activities need not be judged seriously criminal – warrants may be issued for unspecified purposes. It is not fantastical to suggest that having a drink in a pub with a suspected IRA sympathiser could allow for authorised interception of a mobile phone, as could submission of an incorrect tax return.

The definition of serious crime is also objectionable. Here, the offence under investigation must involve violence, substantial gain or 'common purpose' or alternatively be liable to at least three years' imprisonment. Surely, if a serious crime does not lead to that level of sentence, then it should never lead to this level of intrusion. The phrase 'common purpose' is equally disturbing. It could mean a criminal conspiracy, but it could just as easily be interpreted to mean a collective protest. This leads to the frightening image of demonstrators having their phones tapped and e-mail intercepted and their comings and goings recorded merely because they had come together in a legitimate democratic organisation.

There is a need for clear and detailed rules which specifically define the category of people liable to have their telephone tapped, the offences which might provoke such an order, the procedure for drawing up summary reports of conversations, and the circumstances in which recordings or tapes may or should be destroyed. The theoretical suspect who spends the afternoon protesting in Trafalgar Square, has a drink with an Irish friend (suspected of links with terrorist organisations), then fills out his tax return incorrectly, could have his property tampered with on three grounds. If the suspect is never arrested for any crime, he will never know; if arrested and acquitted, he has no redress.

The supervision of such cases is not subject to adequate judicial review. The Home Office consultation paper proposes the maintenance of the current system of a commissioner and a tribunal. The commissioner oversees the actions of the home secretary and is appointed by the prime minister. The only permissible complaint to the tribunal by a citizen is limited to the validity of the warrant. The tribunal is conducted amid a shroud of secrecy as opaque as the subject matter under its jurisdiction. It is held in secret, it does not hear argument, it does not give reasons for any decision. At the time of writing, no complaint had yet been upheld. Although the European Court has described this procedure restrictive, it did not condemn it outright. But recent cases have shown an increased willingness to consider individual civil rights when balancing notions of fairness.

The secretary of state may issue a warrant for telephone interference. It is well established that prior judicial sanction by an impartial judiciary is preferable to the executive authorisation of a warrant. The Labour government's argument is that there is a need for the executive to issue warrants applied for on national security grounds. Yet telephone tapping is surely serious enough to be considered by a judge, as it is in France and Germany, rather than a politician or a police officer. The decision as to whether interference is warranted now depends entirely on subjective assessment by the executive branch of government. This is untenable. Excessive and unwarranted interference should be dealt with by a more independent tribunal so that redress is afforded the individual whose privacy is intruded upon.

During the 1996 House of Lords debate on the extension of the Security Services Act, a Conservative member said that 'a definition (of serious crime) would distract us from our task and create loopholes that could be exploited by unscrupulous defence lawyers to challenge the legality of the security services involvement in a particular case'. The zeitgeist then was to prefer the efficacy of the police and security services to the rights of the individual. The spirit of today's government is to champion human rights, yet this proposed legislation will only extend and entrench pre-existing policies.

Back in 1765, Mr Entick's eloquent lawyer pleaded: 'If they [the search warrants] have been granted by the minister, then it is high time to put an end to them; for if they are held to be legal, the liberty of the country is at an end. Ransacking a man's secret drawers and boxes to come at evidence against him is like racking a body to come at his secret thoughts.' And he won, on the basis that it was unacceptable for an executive to issue warrants authorising intrusion into property. Yet, early in the new millennium, legislation will be introduced which a judge found offensive more than 200 years ago. That our freedom to speak and write through any manner or means can be so fundamentally interfered with, that redress is so limited and that public debate has been so scant, must be cause for concern. ❏

Lisa Forrell is a barrister and theatre director

The new slavery

The slave won't go away, even in a world where consumer choice is paramount. *Index* looks at the undying contribution that slavery still makes to our lives and maps some new metaphors for the old shackles

File compiled by Michael Griffin

KEVIN BALES

Throwaway people

Far from vanishing, the slave is back on the map of the new century – stripped of the few threads of dignity he had 200 years ago

Just when you thought slavery could be relegated to theme parks in Virginia or West Africa, it comes back to haunt. Slavery refuses to die. Though most of us have a fixed idea of 'slavery' as the Atlantic slave trade of 200 years ago, slavery itself keeps changing and growing. It is like tuberculosis: as long as governments are vigilant, the infection is in retreat but, let down your guard, and up pop new drug–resistant varieties in unexpected places. For thousands of years humans have been finding ways to enslave each other but, with typical conceit, western countries decided it had stopped when *they* declared an end to the Atlantic trade. The cycles of self–congratulation that continue today only blind us to the slavery all around. Making slavery illegal doesn't make it disappear.

Of course, if you insist on defining slavery as 'the legal ownership of one person by another', then slavery has pretty well disappeared. But the key is not ownership, but control through violence. In the 5,000 years of human civilisation, slavery has been a constant, sometimes as a form of ownership, sometimes not. Part of our ignorance rests on this confusion about what slavery is.

When most people decided that 'slavery' had disappeared, the word itself went up for grabs. Within the UN, prostitution, incest, even the traffic in transplant organs have been termed slavery. Third–world debt and the emotional condition of women who love too much are 'slavery'. These things are bad enough as they are; they don't *need* to be described as slavery. But with this dilution of meaning, slavery is now everything and nothing.

To help us see who really is a slave we need to remember that there is an irreducible core to slavery: violence. The control of one person by another through violence (or its threat) is the constant attribute of slavery throughout history. Couple that with an economic exploitation in which someone is paid nothing and you have a good working definition of the new slavery that encompasses about 27 million people around the world.

Like other human relationships, slavery isn't static. No one expects marriage to be the same today as it was in 1850; even its legal basis has dramatically altered. Slavery also evolves, but most of us never notice. Modern slavery differs from the past in one special way: slaves today are cheaper than ever in human history. In the same way that mass production lowered the cost of what we buy, overpopulation has made slaves plentiful, cheap and disposable. Most of this change has occurred since WWII, with the world population tripling to 6 billion in 50 years. Rising populations don't cause slavery but, when these new billions are pushed into precarious lives through environmental decline, war, government by kleptocrats or 'structural adjustment', they become the vulnerable prey of slave-hunters. If slavers can act with impunity, if government is sufficiently corrupt or complicit, then the poor can be enslaved.

With the large numbers of vulnerable people and the low cost of violence, slaves are inexpensive. In 1850, an average agricultural slave in Alabama sold for US$1,000, around US$40,000 in today's money. The new owner expected a bill of sale and legal title. The profit made from a slave varied between 5% and 10%, so the slaveholder had to balance the violence needed to control the slave against the risk of an injury that would reduce profits. One result was a long-term relationship between slave and master as owners sought good returns on their investment.

The profits that are made today are obscenely high, without needing to keep slaves healthy. It costs about US$2,000 to enslave a young woman into a brothel in Thailand. Once there she will generate as much as US$75,000 profit each year. She won't be able to keep that up for more than four or five years since HIV is widespread among the men who use her. But the purchase price is low, the profits high and she can be easily replaced if she is ill, injured or just troublesome. Today's slaves are disposable.

Here are a few differences between old and new slavery:

Old Forms of Slavery	New Forms of Slavery
Legal ownership asserted	Legal ownership avoided
High purchase cost	Low purchase cost
Low profits	High profits
Shortage of potential slaves	Surplus of potential slaves
Long-term relationship	Short-term relationship
Slaves maintained	Slaves disposable
Ethnic differences important	Ethnic differences not important

At US$2,000 the young woman in a Thai brothel is one of the world's more costly slaves. People, especially children, can be enslaved today for as little as US$45. The 11-year-old boy I met in India six weeks ago had been placed in bondage by his parents in exchange for about US$35. He now works 14 hours a day, seven days a week making *beedi* cigarettes. This lad is held in 'debt bondage', one of the most common variations on the theme of slavery. Debt bondage is slavery with a twist. Instead of being property, the slave is collateral. The boy and all his work belong to the slaveholder as long as the debt is unpaid, but not a penny from his work is applied to the debt. Until his parents find the money, this boy is a cigarette-rolling machine, fed just enough to keep him at his task. People may be enslaved in the name of religion, like the *Devadasi* of India or the *trokosi* of West Africa. They may be enslaved by their own government, like the hundreds of thousands of people identified by the International Labour Organisation in Burma. Whoever enslaves them, and through whatever trickery, false contract, debt or kidnap method, the reality for the slave is much the same.

While the central theme of slavery is control through violence, that theme is played out in a number of ways. The conditions in which slaves live around the world vary enormously, though under new slavery they are becoming more alike. In those places which still practise a kind of chattel slavery, like Mauritania, there are long-term, often lifelong relationships between master and slave. Sometimes these take on a mutual dependence and genuine affection, however tinged by the unequal power relationship. In most countries, however, the state of slaves is more precarious.

Much depends on the age at which a person is enslaved. The recently freed 22-year-old woman I met in Paris was about eight or nine when she was taken from Mali and enslaved as a domestic. Though she was clearly intelligent, her understanding of the world was less developed than a five-year-old's. Until freed she had no real understanding of time. She had no knowledge of weeks, months or years, only the daily round of work and sleep. She knew that some days were hot and others cold, but she did not know there was a pattern to this called 'seasons'. If she once had known her birthday, she had forgotten it, as well as the concept of 'year' and was confused by the idea of 'ageing'. She was baffled by the idea of 'choice'. Her foster family tried to help her make choices, but she still couldn't grasp the concept.

I asked her to draw the best picture of a person she could. She told me it was the first time she had ever tried to draw a person. The result is a picture an educational psychologist might expect from a four-year-old:

For slaves who have a life *before* enslavement, there is both more and less to lose. Slavery is more painful when you know the alternative, yet at the same time notions of dignity and morality can be used to control you. For example, the very rules of trust and honesty which many poor Brazilians use to guide their dealings with each other are used to enslave them. Many bonded workers I meet have a very strong sense that debts *must* be repaid. Using trickery and taking advantage of this integrity is cheaper than violence and achieves greater productivity. A priest who works with families in the Brazilian charcoal camps told me a story.

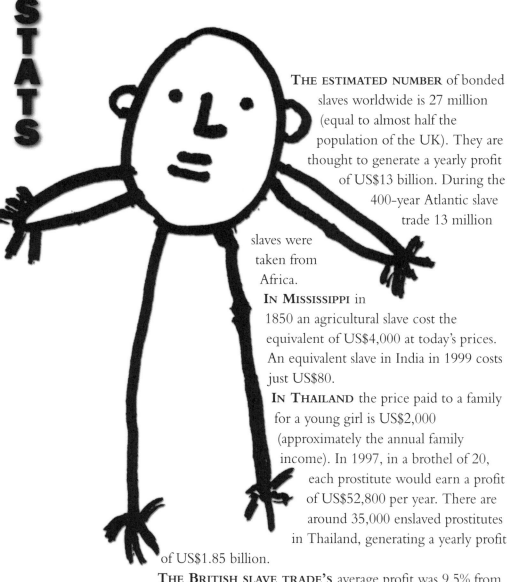

STATS

THE ESTIMATED NUMBER of bonded slaves worldwide is 27 million (equal to almost half the population of the UK). They are thought to generate a yearly profit of US$13 billion. During the 400-year Atlantic slave trade 13 million slaves were taken from Africa.

IN MISSISSIPPI in 1850 an agricultural slave cost the equivalent of US$4,000 at today's prices. An equivalent slave in India in 1999 costs just US$80.

IN THAILAND the price paid to a family for a young girl is US$2,000 (approximately the annual family income). In 1997, in a brothel of 20, each prostitute would earn a profit of US$52,800 per year. There are around 35,000 enslaved prostitutes in Thailand, generating a yearly profit of US$1.85 billion.

THE BRITISH SLAVE TRADE'S average profit was 9.5% from 1761 to 1807. In 1997 the average profit of a Thai brothel of enslaved prostitutes was 856%.

THE NUMBER OF TOURISTS visiting Thailand rose from 2 million in 1981 to 4 million in 1988 and 7 million in 1996, nearly 5 million of whom were unaccompanied men. Sex tourists spend an estimated US$26.2 billion a year – 13 times more than Thailand earns from any one of its major industries. By 2001 4.3 million Thais will be HIV positive.

AN ENSLAVED BRAZILIAN charcoal worker earns US$180–US$270 a month. One charcoal installation makes US$90,000 profit a year.

SLAVERY WAS ABOLISHED in the British Empire in 1838, in Brazil in 1888, in Burma in 1929, in Saudi Arabia in 1962 and in Mauritania in 1980.

IN MAURITANIA a young male slave costs US$500–US$700. A mature female is priced US$700–US$1,000. Young females cost much more.

AT LEAST 100,000 NEPALESE MEN, women and children of low caste ethnic groups are trapped through debt bondage into a lifetime of hard labour just to pay the interest on amounts as little as US$32.

AN ESTIMATED 20 MILLION SLAVES are in debt bondage in Pakistan, despite the banning of the practice in 1992 and assurances that it will stop by 2003.

OVER 1 MILLION GIRLS under the age of 18 work as domestics in the Philippines (population 70 million). The girls are separated from their families, often unpaid and on call 24 hours a day.

IN BURMA during 1997 and 1998 up to 800,000 people a day were forced into hard labour, building for the government or portering for the army.

IN ONE AREA OF THE SOUTH OF SUDAN, 3,000 children from a Christian population of 150,000 were abducted during 1998 to serve as labourers.

FROM 1997 TO 1998 thousands of young girls, aged six to 12, were recruited to work as domestic servants, farm labourers and market vendors and taken from their homes in Togo and neighbouring Benin to other countries in Central and West Africa.

CITIZENS OF 74% OF COUNTRIES with high international debt load are regularly trafficked into slavery (the figure for countries with low international debt load is 29%). In 50% of countries with high international debt load slavery is a regular feature of their economy, compared with just 12% of countries with low international debt load. ❏

Compiled by **Kevin Bales** *and* **Humfrey Hunter** *from various sources*

'It is not always the case that there are people with guns holding workers in the camps. They use something that the poor Brazilian people have: the feeling that they must pay their debts. We had a case of one family which was able to hitch-hike with one of the charcoal trucks to Minas to go to a funeral. And then they came back! I asked: "Why did you come back?" And they said: "Because we owe 800 *reals*. We had to come back and try to pay it." So I told them: "You know you are being robbed of much more than 800 *reals* ($430)." But they just said: "A debt is a debt and we have to pay."'

The UN has been wholly ineffective in stopping slavery. It is not for want of a mandate. There are more than 300 international treaties dealing with slavery and a number of UN conventions specifically concern it. Most countries in the world have signed these conventions. The UN has a Working Group on slavery that meets yearly – but it has no permanent staff. The group spent the Cold War as a political football (both West and East denied anything like slavery existed in *their* spheres), but has since lapsed into bureaucratic lethargy. As the UN Commission on Human Rights grows, and human rights climbs higher on the world's agenda, the issue of slavery unaccountably languishes. Yet what more fundamental violation of human rights exists?

Today the UN normally appoints a Special Rapporteur when it wants to concentrate attention on an issue. There is a Special Rapporteur on torture, for example, and one on violence against women. No full-time person is assigned to slavery. Throughout 1999 the UN Security Council maintained economic sanctions against Iraq, occasionally bombing targets to keep up the pressure. Earlier UN inspection teams searched the country for chemical and biological weapons. But what country has been sanctioned by the UN for slavery? Where are the UN inspection teams charged with rooting out slavery?

The failure to confront slavery is not due to the opposition of vested interests as in the 19th century, when slaves represented a vast capital investment in the American South. Slaves today barely show on the economic map. Even given the high level of profit, the income generated by the total number of slaves is estimated at US$13 billion, roughly equal to what the Dutch spent last year on tourism. Slavery escapes our notice because it is worth so little. If western jobs were threatened, if multinationals were undercut by slave-based enterprises, the alarms would sound. Instead there is the silence of the complicit.

For the most part slaves work at the most basic of tasks: mining, logging, farming, begging, hauling goods, breaking stone, herding and prostitution. But their labour feeds into our economies, and into our pockets. In western Brazil I watched enslaved workers devastating the native forest and then burning it to make charcoal. Charcoal is a key ingredient in Brazil's steel production, the country's second-largest export. The steel goes into everything from toys to skyscrapers, but especially cars and furniture. We enjoy a lower price for these goods because of the slave input. And while it is subcontractors that enslave the charcoal workers, the land on which they work is often owned by major Brazilian and international companies, the kind that figure in investment and pension funds.

Once swept into slavery, a slave has few allies. The fact that slavery emerges most often when governments and police are corrupt eliminates any hope of rescue by the authorities. Anti-Slavery International, the oldest human rights organisation in the world and a massive influence in the 19th century, is now reduced to some 5,000 regular supporters and a level of funding that barely allows it to scratch the surface of slavery. At the grass-roots are organisations which take direct action to liberate and rehabilitate slaves, but in most countries they act in the face of opposition from their governments. Staff often have to fight police, the threat of false arrest and persecution in addition to the slaveholders. Some have brought freed slaves into their organisations but, for the most part, fighting slavery is a top-down operation.

The abolition movements of the past had powerful witnesses in escaped slaves such as Frederick Douglass and Harriet Tubman. The voices of the slaves, today, are seldom heard, even after they have been liberated. Most have missed out on education. They rarely speak any of the 'global' languages and require go-betweens to communicate with the wider world. The silencing of today's slaves relies on a combination of censorship and collusion – from governments, media, ourselves – but sometimes even by the very charities trying to help them. In part this is because of their 'management' by the press and NGOs. Slaves with a voice of their own are about as welcome as refugees with opinions. Both would require us to examine our self-ordained roles as the generous and beneficent. Some charities also have clear notions of how slaves should behave. I was told by a worker who helps to rehabilitate freed slaves for a southern European organisation that her bosses had vetoed research on how the slaves felt about their rehabilitation. 'We know best,' she was told, 'after all, *we* set *them* free.' Charities, sometimes, prefer their slaves co-operative, grateful – and photogenic.

For the media, slaves must be victims. As one television executive said as we discussed his ideas for an 'intellectual' documentary on modern slavery: 'But can't we get film of someone in chains being whipped?' Even media people who seem motivated by the desire to expose slavery are prepared to exploit slaves as they build their own reputations. Perhaps the best example is the treatment of women kidnapped or tricked from eastern Europe into prostitution in the West. In special reports and documentaries we see them, ghoulish in stark night filming, propping up doorways in the seedy underworld of Berlin or Prague. On screen they break down in sobs as they describe their plight, or direct hardened stares as the film crew crawls the kerb. Either way, they are rendered as powerless by film-makers as they have been by their pimps. The clients who make the whole business possible are rarely pursued or questioned though they enjoy 'liberated' sex lives through the slavery of others.

The enslavement of women from eastern Europe and south-east Asia raises thorny questions about freedom of expression. Four of the 10 channels available on one satellite package in Britain are sex channels. European and Asian 'sex workers' are regulars on their programmes. The channels themselves are marketed as liberating alternatives to conservative sexual mores. But how much is this liberal market in sex TV based on the enslavement of others? We oppose censorship, but do we do so at the price of slave-enhanced programming?

Slavery is also the subject of censorship around the world. Many countries claim that they are 'slave-free' when they are clearly not. In India declarations by state governments that that they have eradicated debt bondage within their borders have sapped the struggle to liberate other bonded workers. Under Indian law a freed bonded labourer is entitled to compensation and a rehabilitation grant. But when states are 'slave free', local officials are loath to sully their record by reporting workers in bondage. A young lawyer in Uttar Pradesh thought he would have a quiet life when he was appointed to the state 'vigilance committee', monitoring slavery; after all, the state had declared it had none. Led by local activists, he soon found whole villages in debt bondage, working in quarries, and so began a legal campaign for their recognition. In Brazil there is a government-sponsored 'Potemkin

Village' housing ex-slave charcoal workers in ideal conditions. The handful who live there are over the moon, but they know it is only for show. The US and France collude in Mauritania's assertion that slavery has been eradicated, since they hope to retain Mauritania as a buffer state protecting Black Africa from the Muslim fundamentalists to the north.

In 1852, preparing for the big Fourth of July celebrations, the city-fathers of Rochester, New York, thought to ask Frederick Douglass, one of their more famous citizens, to give the key-note speech. An escaped slave from the South, he had become a leader of the abolitionists. If the city-fathers expected Douglass to be grateful, they were in for a surprise. Douglass mounted the platform and spoke:

'What to the American slave is your Fourth of July? ... a day that reveals to him more than all other days, the gross injustice and cruelty to which he is a constant victim ... your celebration is a sham; your boasted liberty an unholy licence; your national greatness, swelling vanity; ... your denunciation of tyrants, brass-fronted impudence; your shouts of liberty and equality, hollow mockery; your prayers and hymns, your sermons and thanksgivings, your religious parade are ... bombast, fraud, deception, impiety and hypocrisy.'

He poured into the ears of his audience biting ridicule and sarcasm, beneath which lay a single simple question: If there are still slaves how can you be proud of your freedom? We have to answer the same question. Whether we like it or not, we are now global people. Are we willing to live in a world with slaves? If not, we are obligated to take responsibility for things that are connected to us, even when they are far away. Not to take action is simply to give up and let other people jerk the strings that tie us to slavery. There are many forms of exploitation in the world, many kinds of injustice and violence. But slavery is exploitation, violence, and injustice rolled into one. What good is our economic and political power, if we can't use it to free slaves? If we cannot choose to stop slavery, how can we say we are free? ❏

Kevin Bales is a lecturer in sociology at the University of Surrey, Roehampton. His book, Disposable People: New Slavery in the Global Economy, *was published by the University of California Press in 1999*

ALI HASSAN

Slaves, not partners

Laws are in place in Pakistan to bring the practice of bonded labour to an end, but the interests of feudal landlords override them

Ask a *zamindar* (agricultural landlord) about freeing his bonded labourers and his reply will always be the same – 'Oh, you cannot take them without clearing the debt against them.' They all say the same thing. Bonded labour is illegal in Pakistan but, in the eyes of the *zamindar*, it's not slavery but an age-old tradition. And anyway, who cares about the law? The *zamindar* think they're immune.

If it really is a tradition, however, it is not one that is practised throughout the country. Bonded labour prevails in the lower part of the province of Sindh – in the districts of Hyderabad, Thatta, Badin, Sanghar, Mirpurkhas, Umerkot and Nawabshah. In other parts of the province local tribes are so strong that the fear of tribal conflict is enough to put the *zamindar* off the idea of the bonded worker.

Those who fall prey to the bonded labour system are poor families of *haris* (peasants) who have migrated to irrigated areas during periods of drought or famine, desperate for work. Despite land reforms in 1963 and 1973, the *zamindar* own most of the cultivated land and the poor are easy pickings. They take anyone, irrespective of age, gender, physique or religion. The majority of bonded labourers are non-Muslims (*kohli*, *bheel* and other schedule caste Hindus), but Muslims are also victims. Minorities, especially those belonging to a lower class, are dealt with contempt – there is no one to speak up on their behalf.

Appointed to work by a *zamindar*, labourers are given some money as advance payment, but this is the only wage they will ever receive. From this moment on the *hari* becomes bonded labour, held almost in perpetuity, working to pay off a debt which somehow never shrinks.

The managers and *munshis* (supervisors) who work for the *zamindars* maintain this status quo through a variety of means. They never keep their account books up to date. They make debit entries against peasants without providing any receipts or details. When labourers or their families fall ill, charges and expenses, usually inflated, for any medical treatment they receive are debited in the accounts without the consent or knowledge of the labourers. Debits keep on accumulating and become so heavy that the peasants fail to clear them even after discharging their duties working on the season's crop.

Until the so-called debt against them is cleared, labourers are not allowed even to leave the farm where they work. And the debt is only cleared if they are sold, without their consent, to another *zamindar*. Sometimes you can find three generations on one farm working in bondage. Sometimes they are kept in chains, under the surveillance of armed guards. Although the *zamindar* provides his labourers with food, there is never enough of it – a handful of flour is all each family gets. As a result the *hari* suffers from malnutrition. They have no opportunity for rest or leisure periods or holidays.

Of course, it's not meant to be like this. Under the Sindh Tenancy Act of 1950, passed by the provincial assembly after hundreds of *haris* had laid siege to their building, any *zamindar* can engage *haris* as 'partners', entitled to an equal share in the crops they produce. In practice, however, labourers are denied their rightful share – fair accounts are not maintained and nobody monitors the interests of the *hari*.

According to the law, *zamindars* must also enter into a written agreement with labourers and register this with the regional *mukhtiarkar* (an official who collects revenue). Few *zamindars* comply, however. None of them operate according to the 1950 act and nobody takes action against them.

Labourers have little chance to seek redress against their oppressors. The Sindh Tenancy Act gives a *hari* the right to file complaints before a tribunal, headed by *mukhtiarkar*. But if they try the labourers always fail – the official never pays their protests any attention and affords them no respect. The *mukhtiarkar* serve the interests of the *zamindars*.

Any progress that has been made on the behalf of bonded labourers is hard to enforce. Bonded labourers working on brick kilns forced the

Human Rights Commission of Pakistan (HRCP) to change the law in 1992. As a result of their protests the National Assembly of Pakistan passed the Bonded Labour Abolition Act. The law authorises district magistrates to operate and execute the law through his administration and police. But this hasn't helped the *hari* – like the *mukhtiarkar,* the police generally support the *zamindar.*

Even if bonded labourers are freed, they can be kidnapped or recaptured. In September 1998, Mureed Khan Marri, a landlord with a large landholding, took over 150 armed men and attacked a camp of bonded labourers who had been released by activists from his private jail. He kidnapped 87 of them, including women and children, and crossed through three districts and dozens of police posts. No one stopped him.

Pressure mounted by HRCP and the media forced police to set the kidnapped free and Mureed Khan was named when the case was registered at Matli police station. The police, however, have avoided taking action against him – he is an influential *zamindar* in the province. Their inaction has confused people: does the rule of law exist in Pakistan or not? The law applies differently to the rich and poor. Other *zamindar* have also started kidnapping freed labourers.

In Pakistan, whether working on agricultural land, in industrial units or private educational institutions, labourers and employees are exploited and laws flagrantly ignored. The problem lies not with legislation but with those responsible for administering the law. The palms of government functionaries are greased by interested parties who want them to ignore the interests of labourers. The labourers who are meant to work in partnership with the *zamindas* end up, in the south at least, being not partners but slaves. ❏

Ali Hassan *is a stringer for the BBC and a trustee of the Human Rights Commission of Pakistan in Sindh*

IT'S A MYTH THAT

THIRD WORLD LABOUR IS CHEAP. IN MANY CASES, IT'S FREE

CHILD LABOUR IS ILLEGAL UNDER most international laws. In reality, poverty and debt have driven many parents to give their children away. The result? Millions of children working up to 18 hours a day. Weaving carpets. Breaking stones in quarries. Making cigarettes. Frequently beaten. Sent away from home to work as domestic servants. Stranded on dangerously unsafe, fishing platforms. Help us in our fight to combat child labour. Please send a donation.

Advertising space generously donated by Index on Censorship

✂ ------------------------------------

SLAVERY STILL EXISTS. HELP US ABOLISH IT.

I enclose a donation of: ☐ £300   ☐ £100   ☐ £50

☐ £25   ☐ Other £_____

☐ I enclose a cheque/postal order/CAF Voucher made payable to **Anti-Slavery International.**   ☐ Please debit my credit card

☐ Visa   ☐ Mastercard   ☐ CAF   ☐ Amex

Card no. ☐☐☐☐ ☐☐☐☐ ☐☐☐☐ ☐☐☐☐

Expiry date ☐☐/☐☐   Signature_____

Name_____

Address_____

_____ Postcode_____

Thank you for your support.   Registered Charity 1049160

Please send this coupon with your donation to:

anti-slavery
today's fight for tomorrow's freedom

Toral Shah, Anti-Slavery International, Freepost LON10246, London SW9 9BR. Visit our website: www.antislavery.org

HANNANA SIDDIQUI

The ties that bind

When a woman is forced into marriage, she can enter the same legal twilight as a slave

Rukhsana Naz, a 19-year-old, British-born woman of Asian origin, died in Derby in 1998. Her brother ritualistically strangled her with a ligature while her mother held her down by her feet. In court, her mother reportedly said 'it was her *kismit* (fate)'. Her brother claimed provocation – a cultural defence – arguing that the killing was committed in the name of 'honour'.

Rukhsana was murdered for 'shaming her family' by refusing to stay in a marriage to the man who had been chosen for her. She had decided to return to the man she loved and by whom she was pregnant at the time of her death. Under the pretext of reconciliation, her family lured Rukhsana home in order to execute her. They had even prepared the body bag in which she was later buried.

Rukhsana paid heavily for her defiance. Her case may be at the extreme end of the spectrum, but many other Asian women in the UK face cruel treatment for refusing to conform to family expectations. Forced marriage is not confined to Muslim women, but cuts across faith, age, class, caste and racial group. Southall Black Sisters largely focuses on Asian girls and women, but research is needed to ascertain how far other communities are affected. There are no national statistics, but SBS deals with about 1,500 cases and enquiries per year.

Many of these concern forced marriage, which largely remains a hidden problem. Until recently, the British aristocracy practised arranged marriages, many of which were, no doubt, forced. But the institution is still prevalent in the Indian subcontinent and among the diaspora, though the forms it takes vary and changes have occurred. Our parents had little or no choice, but the new generation has more room for negotiation.

Many Asians are forced into marriage under the guise of tradition. Arranged marriages can be consensual, but others are a form of sexual slavery. Numerous pressures are brought to bear, including mental torture and emotional blackmail, actual and threatened violence, rape by their husbands and others within the family, abduction, unlawful imprisonment, the denial of money, controls on dress, movement and rights of association and the denial of education or career opportunities.

Men can be forced into marriage, but it is a practice which overwhelmingly affects women, whose 'sexual purity' represents the honour of the family. Though justified by cultural and religious values, it is an abuse of women's human rights and a means of reducing them to a position of sexual subservience. The stigma attached to women who refuse to marry is so much greater than for men, who not only have more choice over their sexual partners, but greater freedoms without social consequences. For women, the consequences of refusal are family rejection, social ostracism, sexual harassment and acts of sexual violence. And, sometimes, murder.

In August 1998, the UK government established a Home Office Working Group on forced marriage. It was an unprecedented move since the state has always tended to allow minority communities to police themselves. The politics of multi-culturalism does not allow for outside intervention: interference is considered intolerant, even racist. Although Asian women's groups have raised the issue of forced marriage for years, the government only responded after the scandal of the Rukshana Naz case and of another high-profile case involving a mixed-race couple (a white English man and an Asian woman) who went on the run when the woman's family refused to accept their relationship. For several years they were pursued by the family, who used violence against the couple and attempted to track them through professional agencies, 'bounty hunters' and male networks within the community.

Michael O'Brien, the Home Office minister responsible for the working group, has condemned forced marriage and acknowledged that 'multi-culturalism is no excuse for moral blindness'. However, true to the spirit of multi-cultural politics, O'Brien and the government have declared that community leaders must resolve the problem themselves. The fact that they are mostly male, conservative, orthodox or even fundamentalist (and not in Islam alone) seems to have escaped the government. Women are invisible and silenced. Their views are censored by the very same leaders who act as mediators between the community, the state and wider society. It is unlikely that they will surrender their power base and support women's struggles.

Although SBS is a member, until recently the Working Group largely consulted community leaders and conservative Asian women's organisations. Last November, we organised a consultation meeting in Southall, the first in which the Working Group heard directly from women who had gone through, or escaped from, forced marriage. As a result, the Working Group is beginning to consult the more radical Asian women's groups, though what weight will be given to their views remains a concern.

Will the Working Group deliver? Success depends on whose voices are considered legitimate: those of community leaders, or of women? Who and what will the state censor? Will it pursue a policy of appeasement of men and community leaders for the sake of 'good community and race relations', or listen to the voices of minority women and take on board their demands. If it listens to women, it will challenge the community leaders, male power, as well as racism and the multi-cultural policies, which currently deny women their rights to the state's protection.

These challenges are highlighted by one of our current cases. 'Rubina' (her name has been changed) is imprisoned under armed guard by an uncle in Pakistan, who regularly subjects her to violence and rape. Her father, other members of her family and several community leaders in both the UK and Pakistan colluded in her abduction from the UK and the abuse she suffered both here and abroad. Her crime? She refused to be forced into marriage and married instead a man of her own choosing. Rubina's husband is now in hiding in the UK, unable to travel to Pakistan to rescue his wife because of threats against his life from her family.

The husband approached the police several months before he contacted SBS. When asked what action they had taken, they said, besides contacting Interpol, they had done nothing because of 'other operational priorities, such as robberies'. We went for assistance to John Grieve at the Racial and Violent Crime Task Force at New Scotland Yard, established in the wake of the Stephen Lawrence inquiry. Although this led to more co-operation from the police, they said that there was little they could do since most of the crimes had been committed outside their jurisdiction. It will be interesting to see if they will pursue charges for the assault and imprisonment of Rubina in the UK prior to her abduction, or use their powers to rescue a crucial witness who has been unlawfully taken abroad.

The Foreign and Commonwealth Office also failed to offer effective help. A UK citizen who had never formally taken on Pakistani nationality, Rubina, we are informed, is regarded as a dual national upon return to the country of her parents' origin. Rubina has begged the British Consulate by telephone for help, only to be told that it can do nothing unless she escapes and travels to the High Commission in person. Is this the response when white British nationals are held hostage abroad?

British racism and cultural relativism deny Asian women the right to universal human rights – a principle Britain criticises other countries for failing to adhere to. However, it seems that good diplomatic relations – like good community relations – are maintained at the expense of women's lives. ❏

Hannana Saddiqui *is joint co-ordinator and case worker at Southall Black Sisters, founded 1979. For further information, write to 52 Norwood Road, Southall, Middlesex, UB2 4DW*

HARRY WU

Slaves to the state

A convicted prisoner surrenders his right to freedom. At what point does he also surrender the value of his labour?

Systems of slave labour continue to exist in China. As a survivor of the Chinese forced labour camp system – the *Laogai* – I can testify to the excruciating ways in which I was reduced to an instrument of the state and forced to work under deplorable conditions to line the pockets of those in control. Under constant threat of physical and psychological abuse, hundreds of thousands of *Laogai* prisoners continue to be abused to help the Communist government maintain control and profit from the labour of its inmates.

Academics, prisoner rights advocates and the general public continue to argue that the US also allows prison labour and is therefore hypocritical to 'point a finger' at China's forced labour system. Without making excuses for the abuses and inequalities that persist in the US prison system, it is vital to draw distinctions between prison labour in the United States and forced labour in China. Only by exploring the ethical issues surrounding the labour of the incarcerated can we establish criteria for what comprises legitimate punishment or what violates recognised standards of human rights.

The fundamental problem of the *Laogai* is the process by which it acquires it victims. Under Chinese justice, the treatment of criminals is archaic and the current power structure has delayed any significant movement to introduce due process or legal reform. Steps have been made to codify procedures, most recently in the 1996 and 1997 revisions to the Criminal Procedure Law and the Criminal Code, but the fundamentals of due process are still nowhere to be found. China lacks the presumption of innocence, admits illegally gathered evidence and uses extra-judicial – so-called 'administrative' – sanctions to circumvent the criminal justice system. Compounding these *de jure* problems is the *de facto* suspension of encoded rights at the whim of the Party. Inequalities exist in the US legal system, evident in the disproportionate number of African–Americans in prison, but there are protections inscribed in law that facilitate an appeals process and allow for claims for wrongful action.

The crackdown on practitioners of the banned Falun Gong movement is a case study in the deficiencies and hypocrisies of the Chinese legal system. Since its formal banning in July, the government is reported to have detained over 35,000 members, sentencing 2,000 to labour camps. Lawyers were instructed not to represent them and incidents of torture have been reported. For these people, there is no recourse, no appeal and no compensation.

China's detention centres, prisons and labour camps are full of victims of its judicial and penal systems: from members of Falun Gong accused of belonging to an illegal cult, to labour and democracy activists charged with the all-encompassing 'threat to state security', to participants of the 1989 Tiananmen Square movement who were charged with the criminal acts of hooliganism or arson, to those who may indeed be guilty of criminal acts, but whose convictions were obtained through coerced confessions and illegally obtained evidence. To brand as unethical the forced labour of prisoners of conscience, or of accused criminals convicted illegally, is a logical conclusion; but the problem in China goes deeper.

To discuss the ethical ramifications of the use of labour by the more general inmate population, as opposed to prisoners of conscience, one must explore one basic question: does the labour deprive the prisoner of his or her humanity? Does the institution which imposes, or provides, the work look upon the prisoner as an individual deserving of a productive way of spending time, or is the prisoner simply a tool to be utilised to his maximum capacity, and often beyond?

According to *Factories with fences*, a 1999 report by the Federal Bureau of Prisons, the purposes of prison labour in the US penal system are to reduce idleness, promote cost–efficiency, provide job–training and rehabilitation and, lastly, to teach the prisoner financial responsibility. The American Civil Liberties Union (ACLU) favours the provision of meaningful work to prisoners, though it remains decidedly wary of the potential for private firms to exploit the labour of hired prisoners, while labour activists criticise the way in which prison labour takes jobs away from the civilian work force.

In China, labour is instituted with a different purpose. *Laogai* translates literally as 'reform through labour'. The fundamental policy of the *Laogai*, according to Mao Zedong, was 'reform first, production second.' At first glance, 'reform' – a more complete version of the more commonly used term 'rehabilitation' – might seem a nobler goal that mere retribution. But history has shown that the state's claim to 'reform' its citizens is nothing more than an attempt to forcefully manipulate individuals into becoming submissive tools of the state, thus bringing into question the legitimacy of 'reform' as an end in itself.

The Communist Party has certainly been no exception. While the intense study sessions of the Maoist era are now a thing of the past, prisoners must still repeatedly confess their crimes and offer self-criticism, as well as renounce any political and religious beliefs that the state considers 'subversive'. Even more common in contemporary China is the melding of 'reform' and labour to produce the desired results: the Communist Party squeezes out every available ounce of labour from its prisoners to prove that they are but tools at the mercy of the state.

If one examines the basic factors that can make labour either fulfilling or dehumanising – hours, conditions and compensation – the intentions of China's forced labour become clear. The brutal regime of labour I endured in my 19 years in prison did little to reform or ennoble me. I survived only by reducing myself to my most primal needs: I became a beast. I have heard the same horrible reality echoed in the stories of other *Laogai* survivors. From Mao's time to the present day, the *Laogai* brings its victims to their knees and then leaves them to crawl.

Prisoners work from nine to 16 hours a day. There are reports of prisoners of conscience quarrying and hauling rocks during the day and then assembling artificial flowers for export long into the early morning. Conditions differ, of course, from camp to camp, but they are generally deplorable. No safety equipment is available for general factory and mining work and prisoners in some camps are forced to mine asbestos, sulphur, coal and work with toxic chemicals to tan

Chain gang prisoner kneeling to be chained, Limestone County Correctional Facility, Limestone County, Alabama, 1995 – Credit: James Nachtwey

hides or produce batteries with no protection whatsoever. Prisoners who fail to meet labour quotas suffer beatings, extended sentences, solitary confinement and deprivation of food. Even the 1992 White Paper on

Criminal Reform, a not-at-all subtle piece of propaganda on the 'progressive nature of China's prison system', proudly admits the need to instill in prisoners the concept of 'no work, no food'. This enlightened system deprives individuals of the basic requirements of subsistence in the service of the goal of 'reform'.

Contrary to official propaganda, it is impossible to find any record of prisoners being compensated for their labour. The only occasion on which there is nominal compensation is in the system of 'forced job placement', known as *jiuye*. In this ingenious programme, prisoners are 'placed' in jobs when they have served their sentence – usually in the same camp in which they were imprisoned. Having been stripped of residence permits for their home towns, these ex-prisoners remain in the same camp under the same brutal conditions as during their sentence.

The sole party to profit from forced labour is the state. The precise scale of forced labour in the Chinese economy is shrouded in secrecy, but Dun & Bradstreet's lists 99 forced labour camps in its 1995/6 *Directory of Key Manufacturing Companies in PR China*. Forced labour is closely integrated with local industry: the *Laogai* produces the steel, cement and wood products used in regional development. A modern prison chemical industry exists, which produces 60% of the nation's rubber vulcanising agent. Prisoners pick the cotton that is used in 'legitimate' clothing manufacturing. *Laogai* prisoners assemble or process garments and toys, exporting these products so that western nations can line their shelves with cheap goods. The circuitous routing of international sub-contracting, import-export companies and the use of dual public and private prison names makes the involvement of the *Laogai* industries in the export business difficult, if not impossible, to trace.

China may be moving towards a market-oriented economy, but the government's view of its citizens has not changed since the time of Mao. Individuals are expendable and worth only as much as they can be made to produce. In a forced labour camp, where individuals are under constant government supervision, it is that much easier to ensure that they are used to their maximum value. ❏

Harry Wu, a former political prisoner in China, is Executive Director of the Laogai Research Foundation, which investigates and disseminates information on systemic human rights abuses in China

PETER VERNEY

Redemption by numbers

US kids are washing windows to free enslaved Sudanese children. Have the Arab slavers returned, or is this the ultimate low in child sponsorship?

'Why is that woman talking to that slave?' This illuminating complaint was attributed to a northern Sudanese opposition politician who felt snubbed when US Secretary of State Madeleine Albright chose recently to meet with John Garang, the southern Sudanese guerrilla leader. It showed the painful gap between the accounts of slavery in southern Sudan that have occupied so much of the media's attention and the grubby reality of everyday prejudice between northern and southern Sudanese. The equivalent of a US politician using the 'N–word' about an African–American colleague, it reveals just how far Sudan has to go if it is to eradicate both the practice of slavery and the lingering attitudes that make it possible.

Since the mid–1990s, reports of the freeing of slaves in 'buy–back' schemes by foreign aid agencies have brought an outpouring of concern – and an opening of wallets – in the West, notably the US. But the apparently simple certainties of fund–raising to purchase the freedom of slaves and blaming the trade solely on the current Sudanese regime are only fragments of a more complex truth. The agencies' protests have also stirred reactions, forcing other humanitarian organisations and the Sudan government itself to put a neglected issue on the agenda. But the vociferousness has provoked a backlash, not only from the regime, but from Sudanese who oppose the regime and from Muslims around the world. There is a propaganda war going here on in which the roots of a different crisis are being obscured.

The revelation that chattel slavery was still operating in south-western Sudan, across the fault-lines of the civil war and as an intrinsic part of that war, took a long time to dawn. A full decade elapsed between the first substantiated report – written by two Muslim Sudanese in 1986 – to the recent coverage in the western media and the emergence of the buy-back approach as a controversy in itself. The slide towards the re-emergence of slavery began under the dictatorship of Jaafar Nimeiri in the late 1970s, but it was kick-started in the mid-1980s by Fadlalla Burma Nasser, defence minister in Sadiq al-Mahdi's elected government. He did not actively promote a policy of 'enslavement' but, by arming Baggara militias as a means of combating the southern rebels, he triggered a wave of cattle raids in which Dinka women and children were abducted for use as farm labourers, domestic servants or for purposes of rape.

Ushari Mahmoud and Suliman Baldo, authors of the 1986 report on the Ad Daien massacre which provided evidence of slavery, were harassed – and Ushari was jailed. Prominent Dinka, notably Bona Malwal, who edited the *Sudan Times*, tried to draw attention to the report but, despite taking maximum advantage of a brief opening of the domestic press, he barely pricked the world's awareness. A correspondent for *Anti-Slavery Reporter*, the magazine of the then Anti-Slavery Society, said that even UNICEF had failed to respond.

The story has only come to prominence since an Islamist dictatorship has been in power in Sudan. The regime of Mohammed Al-Bashir has incorporated human rights abuse into its political methods more ruthlessly than any of its predecessors since independence in 1956. It deployed armed, semi-trained militia to devastate the civilian populations in the Nuba Mountains and the south and east, turning a blind eye when the consequences included slave-taking. But Sudan's 'pariah' status has hinged more on its alleged complicity in international terrorism, especially in US eyes. Now that it is exporting oil for the first time, Sudan is trying to lose that association, and its reputation for human rights abuse. The amnesia is being encouraged by public relations consultants employed by the oil companies.

To keep the memory fresh, some human rights campaigners have identified slavery among the abuses committed to make the region safe for oil development. There have been raids to ethnically cleanse villagers, in which slaves were reportedly taken, but slavery is not the main issue.

There is a danger in overemphasising it because it shocks more than a helicopter gunship raid or the less vivid idea, 'human rights violations'. Slavery distracts from the demonstrably deliberate, systematic and more modern atrocities perpetrated by the National Islamic Front government. Slavery gets ratings, but the way it is reported maintains shorthand fictions in the minds of people who know little else about Sudan, or its Muslim and non-Muslim peoples.

In the US, coverage of slavery in Sudan has been influenced by the religious right, and by domestic perceptions of Islam. These are typified by the demonisation of the African-American leader of the Nation of Islam, Louis Farrakhan. Returning from a visit to Sudan in 1996, Farrakhan was asked what he thought of the emerging accounts of slavery and was invited to condemn the regime for it. He declined, saying he knew of no such evidence. In response, the *Baltimore Sun* assigned two journalists – one white, the other black – to accompany Christian Solidarity International (CSI) workers to witness slaves being 'redeemed'. The jamboree that followed did little to shift attitudes at home: indeed, it tended to feed the prejudices of both sides. For some media, 'slaver' had become a convenient extra epithet to throw in with 'terrorist'.

Despite a more questioning line in 1999, notably by the *Atlantic Journal*, there is still plenty of mileage for slave redemption programmes in the US, where they are defended as the only way to respond to a clear and present need. John Eibner, whose UK group Christian Solidarity Worldwide redeems slaves, claims to have freed 7,725 since 1995. He sees redemption as imperfect but necessary. 'Knowing that tens of thousands of people are still enslaved and knowing that we can get them out,' he said, 'I couldn't live with myself and say: "Sorry, I'm stopping because of some criticism from an ivory tower in London or New York."' His colleague Caroline Cox said: 'We justify it by saying: "It's not the answer, but you can't look a child in the face and say: *I'm sorry, you have to remain a slave until there is a political solution*."'

Critics deride the buy-back schemes as a sop to conscience and the ultimate low in child sponsorship gambits, claiming the average US$50 redemption freedom fee risks generating further slave raiding in a region with no functioning economy. Early NGO estimates of the number of Sudanese slaves ranged up to 6,000, a figure that is well exceeded by the 15,000 that agencies claim to have already 'bought back'.

'Once the numbers started to increase drastically, that caused people who follow the slavery issue to have a look at what is really going on,' Jemera Rone, counsel for Human Rights Watch in Washington, told the *New York Times* early this year. Rone worries that unscrupulous middlemen – the traders who bring the slaves back south – may increase profits by packing groups of slaves with 'borrowed' children, and that peace in Sudan may be discouraged if raiders have a new financial incentive to keep the war going.'

Media debate inevitably pits critics and supporters of buy-back against one other, with supporters leaning heavily on the emotional response to a child's loss of freedom. All those American kids cleaning windscreens to free slaves in Sudan are presented as if a display of good intentions excused the shortcomings of the response. A similar fascination for the slavery exists in Europe. News of the sabotage of the new pipeline pumping oil through the ethnically cleansed areas of Sudan, though profound in its implications, had a fraction of the coverage that slavery has attracted.

For their part, Muslims hold to an array of views on slavery, variously claiming that Islam outlaws it, sanctions it, transforms it or legalises it. What they don't appreciate is being cornered by disapproving westerners who, they perceive, point accusatory fingers while ignoring their own history of slave trading. The Arab and Muslim press takes exception to the West's implicit 'Arab-terrorist-slaver' label. Its own prejudices are reflected in suspicion of the anti-slavery lobby's motives. Charles Jacobs, founder of the American Anti-Slavery Group in 1993, 'is now credited with being the driving force behind the campaign against slavery in Sudan', asserts Ismail Royer of *www.iviews.com*. He claims that 'Jacobs and other leading figures in the anti-slavery movement have a strong political agenda and a history of activism in support of the state of Israel [including] the National Unity Coalition for Israel (NUCI), an umbrella group of evangelical Christian organisations and far right Jewish groups'. Little sign of dialogue there.

The conciliatory, diplomatic approach has its own pitfalls. In late November, the daily *Al-Khaleej* reported that the resident representative of UNICEF, Thomas Ekvall, 'has affirmed that UNICEF has concluded that the practices which were once termed as slavery are actually cases of abduction in the conflict areas ... The executive director of UNICEF, Ms Carol Bellamy, has apologised for the misunderstanding.' The report referred to the work of the Committee for the Eradication of Abduction of Women and Children, established in late 1998 by the Ministry of Justice with representatives of the Baggara and Dinka and supported by several UN agencies. The acceptance by international agencies of the substitute word 'abduction' for 'enslavement', no doubt in the hope of getting something done, opened a linguistic escape route that the regime jumped at.

But when Ghazi Suleiman, a lawyer who has been in and out of jail for years for pro-democracy activism, can disbelievingly ask a gathering of anti-slavery workers in mid-1999: 'Do you really think we Sudanese buy and sell people?', the depth of northern Sudanese denial couldn't be clearer.

But which comes first: the truth or the reconciliation? ❏

Peter Verney *is editor of* Sudan Update*, an independent information service*

LANDEG WHITE

Pharaohs on the bus

Black Studies remain locked in the charnel house of the Atlantic slave trade, inventing 'pick and mix' histories for the slaves' descendants

It's one thing to abolish slavery. Abolishing its legacy is another matter. I'm not referring to the inheritance of poverty and discrimination, in whatever ex-slave society they may occur. Those problems belong to the arena of political action. I'm writing of the intellectual legacy, the continuing shackles of the questions that refuse to go away.

One of the most striking features of African studies is the contrast between its Southern and West African versions. In West African studies, the main themes are nationalism (pre-colonial empires, colonial resistance, the origins of the modern state) and independence (corruption, warfare, and the new colonialism of the IMF). It's a tale dominated by Africans, the responsibility starting at home. African politicians and generals looted the economy, ruined the country and locked up or murdered the journalists who told the truth. Meanwhile, singers, poets and novelists have entertained us with their skills, refusing to be cowed, and honouring the tribe (no one in West Africa is embarrassed to speak of such matters as 'the Ashanti world-view').

In Southern African studies, by contrast, every theme continues to address the enduring lie of apartheid. No one writes of specifically Zulu or Xhosa cultures because that was 'apartheid language'. No praise poet is revered for his artistry, his game with language, because protest poetry is too urgent for stylistic flourish. As for African responsibility, even in Banda's Malawi it seemed an irrelevance. Six years after apartheid's official demise, it continues to inspire the special pleading that reflects apartheid's agenda. Only slowly, painfully and controversially, are Southern African studies catching up with a broader African agenda.

It ought to be a truism that African studies should be Africa-centred. But in the United States, Black studies (as they are significantly named) remain dominated by the Atlantic slave trade. It's perverse to complain of this. The slave trade was a trade in Africans, and Black studies are inspired by their descendants. Yet it continues to lock scholars into the dispiriting ghetto of asserting what should always have been obvious, and of challenging what was always indefensible. In the process, something quintessentially African gets lost.

Of many possible examples, take, for instance, the growing obsession with Egypt. When Michael Jackson asks his audiences 'Do you remember the time?', he conjures visions of an Egypt ruled by black Pharaohs, centuries in advance of the rest of the world, the origin of all that is best in today's western culture, rich in learning and talent, in gold and silver and slaves – but hang on, what are those slaves doing there?

It's a complicated argument. When the great West Indian-born Liberian writer Edward Wilmot Blyden contemplated the pyramids, he was stirred by the thought 'this was the work of my African progenitors'. But he meant the slaves of the Pharaohs, not the Pharaohs themselves. When the composer of the famous spiritual wrote 'Let my people go', or indeed when Martin Luther King spoke movingly of having glimpsed the Promised Land, they were identifying with the Children of Israel rather than with their Egyptian oppressors.

Three things have turned the argument upside down, over and above the enduring struggle of black American writers and artists to establish their human worth. First, in the 1960s, came the rise of the Black Power movement, and the search for authentically power-exercising origins. Second has been an internalisation of the white American prejudice that anyone with a trace of black blood is black. As *Ebony* editor Lerone Bennet put it, whatever the precise skin colour of ancient Egyptians, they would all of them, Pharaohs included, 'have been forced in the forties to ride on the back seats of the buses in Mississippi'. The third ingredient is the anti-Semitism of certain black Muslim leaders, with the insistence that Jews were implicated in the slave trade and the rejection of the story of the Exodus as a historical analogue. Pharaohs Akhnaten and Amenhotep III have toppled Moses as black role models.

The consequences for the black American understanding of Africa are bizarre. For it is not just, as Blyden put it, that 'those stirring characters ... sent civilisation to Greece'. Egypt is also assumed to be the origin of everything that was best in Africa, civilisation spreading not just north and west to Greece and Rome and London, but south and west from the Nile valley to all parts of the continent. In the process of arguing this, the polemicists concerned – writers like Molefi Asante and Yosef bem-Jochannan – make themselves accomplices of some of the most racially bigoted writing ever produced about Africa.

I'm referring, of course, to the so-called Hamitic theory, the hypothesis that long dominated African studies in Europe, that civilisation in Africa was spread by light-skinned people of Egyptian origin (with well-shaped noses). The story went that, before historical records began, these fanned out across the continent as a ruling elite but subsequently degenerated through intermarriage with primitive peoples. It was a handy theory for invaders and colonists. Everything in Africa that upset the belief in white racist superiority was explained away as being of non-African origin. Hardly surprising that *The Arab Builders of Great Zimbabwe* should be a best-seller in Ian Smith's Rhodesia, when Seligman's *Races of Africa*, arguing that all African achievement from Great Zimbabwe to the Benin bronzes indicated an Arab or Phoenician or Aryan source, was still on sale in London. Seligman's book remains a key text in understanding the colonial mind. But it's weird to trace the line from his belief in the Egyptian source of African ideas of divine kingship to Eddie Murphy's portrayal of an African prince in *Coming to America*.

So we find American Black studies perpetuating the notion that civilisation 'diffused' through Africa from the Nile valley. The famous soapstone birds of Zimbabwe are Egyptian falcons, while the Yoruba of Nigeria, with their superior culture and sophisticated religion, actually migrated from Egypt – providing a neat link with the Shango and Ogun cults in the new world. As for the Hamitic theory's assumption of African degeneracy, Black studies has no difficulty in accommodating that. As Stephen Howe points out in his comprehensive study *Afrocentricism: Mythical Pasts and Imagined Homes*, the last thing Black studies spokespersons are interested in is any contemporary African realities. Meanwhile, the work of the half-mad German anthropologist Leo Frobenius is proclaimed 'an intellectual triumph'. Frobenius, best remembered as a looter of African artefacts, preached that whatever was not of Egyptian origin in West African art derived from the lost continent of Atlantis.

There is, obviously, another version of African history available, pioneered in the 1960s at the universities of Wisconsin and London. That arose in response to the sight of sophisticated African politicians negotiating their countries' independence in London and Paris and taking their seats at the UN. Where had these figures sprung from? Anthropology, still preoccupied with kinship and the tribe, could not explain. The new discipline could, and it has gone from strength to strength, not least in the work of African, Afro-British and Afro-American scholars. Black Studies in America, however, remains locked in the charnel house of the Middle Passage. The intellectual legacy of Atlantic slavery may yet turn out to be its most enduring bondage. ❏

Landeg White has worked in Trinidad, Malawi, Sierra Leone, Zambia and UK and now teaches at the Universidade Aberta in Lisbon. His latest collection of poetry, South, *has recently been published by Cemar*

BRIAN EDWARDS

Lap of the gods

Unable to leave, unpaid, severely exploited and controlled by violence, the *trokosi* are slaves by any other name

About an hour east of Ghana's capital, Accra, lies the Volta delta, a fertile plain criss-crossed by a few metalled roads, and speckled with Ewe villages that have changed little for centuries.

Among the Ewe nothing happens without cause. They are fervent believers in Einstein's maxim that 'God does not play dice'. If someone dies, it is for a reason. There is the superficial cause – malaria, drowning, etc. And there is the profound cause – the displeasure or vengeance of the gods. A family who has experienced notable misfortune – deaths, illness or just a failing crop – may well seek out a soothsayer, a man or woman who can make contact with the spirit world, in order to divine *why* the family has so displeased the gods.

Once the cause of the offence has been divined, the soothsayer will communicate what offering the gods will accept as compensation. According to the elders, for hundreds of years these offerings have comprised cattle, perhaps some rolls of calico and a few crates of the local moonshine, *apeteshe*. Then, around a hundred years ago, an unfortunate change occurred. A family unable to buy the prescribed cattle offered the shrine priest one of their virgin daughters instead. This offer was accepted, and a new tradition was born.

Visiting Ghana for a Channel 4/Home Box Office project, *Innocents Lost*, on the exploitation of children around the world, we filmed several thousand of these women and girls serving at shrines throughout the delta. Called *trokosi* in the Ewe language, they are, in theory, wives and servants to the gods. In practice, their role ranges from the purely ceremonial, to working as the priests' cooks, farmhands, cleaners and mistresses.

In one shrine we were able to speak to some *trokosi* in private while they were working the fields owned by the shrine. Christy was typical. A slight, pretty 12-year-old, her parents had brought her to the shrine two years before. All she knew about her captivity was that her older sister had been a *trokosi* before her, but the *fetish* or god had killed her, so Christy had been sent to replace her. As far as she was aware, she was serving a life sentence for a crime someone else had committed. 'It's for ever,' she told us. 'Even when I die my family will have to bring somebody else and, when she dies, they will bring another person.'

We asked another girl, Atuishe, if she was happy in the shrine. 'Happy? Oh no, I am a *trokosi*, not a normal person. Others live free, but I am suffering in bondage here. If I could have got some poison I would have taken it long ago.'

No one is quite sure how many *trokosi* are enslaved in Ghana, partly because the conditions in which they live vary so much. In some shrines, the priests regard the girls as sexual property and, although they are only supposed to have sex with them 'after their third menstruation', we met several girls who had children by the priests when they were as young as 12.

One girl told us how the priest had come to her in the night when she was just 10. She knew what he wanted but kept refusing to comply. Several nights later he raped her. Afterwards, as she lay on the ground crying, the other girls begged her to be quiet. They warned that if the priest was disturbed he would come back and not only beat her, but beat them as well.

Conversely, in another shrine, the priest, Obosumfor, was appalled when we told him how other priests treated their *trokosi*. He believed that the offer of service made by a family was to the gods, not to him. If a family offered their daughter, he ordered a feast and told them to return in a week's time to celebrate. Obosumfor, his family, the girl and her family would eat and drink late into the night, singing and drumming to attract the gods' attention. As dawn broke he would perform a ritual in which the girl became a *trokosi*. Then, everyone, including the girl, would simply go home. As far as Obosumfor was concerned, the girl would serve the gods in the spirit world (their domain), but would continue a normal life in the material world.

As film-makers we were there primarily as observers. Our plan was not to get involved. Then we met Juliet, a frightened 14-year-old. Her mother had whisked her away from her village to the capital to prevent her in-laws sending the girl to a shrine as a *trokosi*. Ten years earlier, Juliet's father, Joshua, had stolen a tape recorder from his friend, Willie. Willie went to the priest and the priest told Joshua he must return the tape recorder, pay Willie compensation and pay a fine to the shrine. Joshua ignored this ruling and, in so doing, went against the will of gods.

Eight years later Joshua's father and mother died. Two deaths in swift succession sent the family elders scurrying to the soothsayer. He confirmed their worst fears: the gods were angry with the family for ignoring the earlier judgment. Unless the family paid not only the original fine, but also compensation to the shrine in the form of a *trokosi*, the deaths would continue.

We joined Joshua and his family on the way to the shrine to try to negotiate a reduction in the fine, and in particular to try to secure Juliet's freedom. The shrine was a mud hut with a corrugated iron roof in the centre of a village of 20 or so buildings about two hours from the nearest metalled road. The outside was painted with caricatures of the reigning priest's most recent ancestors. The bottles of vodka we had brought as an offering smoothed permission for us to enter the shrine and to film. After a couple of hours of formalities, negotiations began in earnest.

'Negotiation' is an entirely inaccurate description. First Joshua, then each of the relatives who had accompanied him, threw themselves on the earth floor in front of the priest in turn and begged for mercy. Faces pressed into the hard-packed clay, they reached out and touched his feet and asked for the 15 head of cattle to be reduced to five, the five crates of *apeteshe* to be reduced to one, the three rolls of calico to be forgotten.

We had arrived mid-morning. Six hours later the small patch of sunlight that filtered into the shrine through the one opening near the roof was beginning to move up the opposite wall. Negotiations were drawing to a close, yet Juliet's name had not been mentioned.

Finally we asked our interpreter.

'Why haven't they mentioned Juliet?'

'I don't know.'

'Can you ask them why Juliet's freedom has not been discussed.'

The girl, we were told, was not up for negotiation; she had to come to the shrine; it was what the gods wanted.

When we asked if the gods would accept money or cattle in her place, the priest and his acolytes retired for a private conference. When they returned the priest threw his cowrie shells on the floor and

Trokosi field girls, Ghana – Credit: Brian Edwards

considered the pattern before announcing that the gods had decreed that Juliet's freedom could be bought for 5 million Cedis (US$2,415). This was Joshua's entire earnings for about 10 years. Without doubt our presence had massively inflated the price.

We knew the danger of getting involved because we had heard tales of German and US charity workers arriving at shrines laden with donations from church collections to 'free sex slaves in Africa'. Word of these charities spread fast and the number of *trokosi* at any one shrine became increasingly exaggerated. Girls from other villages would be drafted in and several thousand dollars would be handed over, the girls would be 'freed' but the real *trokosi* remained enslaved.

Many priests are vehemently opposed to these liberations. One, Gidisu, threatened to put a curse on any 'liberator' setting foot on his island. He told us all his *trokosi* were very happy, and none of them wanted to leave, but he wouldn't let us speak to them. When we raised the question of cattle in exchange for girls, he was very clear: a girl had a lot more uses than a cow.

After our film and another exposé by ABC's '60 Minutes' were broadcast, the Ghanaian government passed a law in late 1998 making it illegal to send a child away from home for a religious ritual. However, the real challenge is to implement this. In the Volta delta few policemen will act against the priests. Instead elders and chiefs have been recruited to try to persuade priests to give up their girls for cattle.

It was this approach we adopted to try to secure Juliet's freedom. With the help of the local charity, International Needs, Juliet's freedom was secured in exchange for just three cows.

Despite their successes International Needs estimates that there are still up to 3,000 girls living in bondage in the region. Liberations continue but the emphasis now is on getting the priests who have already liberated their *trokosi* to persuade those still holding girls that the game is up. ❏

Brian Edwards is a television producer/director based in London. His 1995 documentary with Kate Blewett, The Dying Rooms, *exposed systematic neglect in China's orphanages. They are currently making a film investigating modern slavery around the world. To find out more about the campaign to free* trokosi *contact International Needs, 9 Station Approach, Funderstead Road, South Croydon, Surrey CR2 0PL*

ALAN HOPE

La ronde

Women are an inexhaustible commodity for the East European *mafiosi* who trade them across borders and between states

If you want to keep your slave docile, you can beat her regularly and savagely, cut her with a knife, drug her, rape her or burn her with cigarettes. On the other hand, if physical violence reduces her value, you can rely on threats to turn her in as an illegal immigrant or a fake refugee, to mutilate or kill her, or to visit some terrible harm on her family.

All of the above techniques are regularly used on slaves being held in western European countries today: the women trafficked from eastern Europe to work for gangs of organised international criminals as prostitutes.

According to estimates from the International Organisation for Migration, as many as half a million such women are brought every year from eastern and central Europe into the European Union. The majority are aged between 18 and 25, but increasing numbers are younger. Some are transported by force, some are aware they are coming to sell themselves, but most are duped.

The illegal nature of trafficking, together with the constant refinement and adaptation of traffickers' methods, makes it difficult to estimate figures. Since the collapse of communism, numbers have been growing, and the commodity refuses to run out. Initially, women came from Poland, Czechoslovakia and Hungary, but now Russia and former Soviet states like Ukraine are the major sources of trafficked women, driven by economic hardship and dreams of a better life in the West.

Trafficking is also a consequence of a reduction in the opportunities for legal migration to the West, says Joanna Maycock, EU liaison officer for the IOM office in Brussels. Albanian women have been turning up in Europe since 1991, according to the IOM, and recent events have made the flood unstoppable. Women are now appearing from Kosovo, though the numbers are confused: many Yugoslavs and Albanian nationals claim to be Kosovars in the hope of receiving more sympathetic treatment from the authorities.

Recruitment varies according to destination. For countries, such as Italy and Switzerland, which still give temporary 'artist' visas, newspaper advertisements call for dancers, hostesses, even strippers. Few of the women who respond expect a career on the streets. For other countries, such as Belgium and the Netherlands, women are recruited to work in domestic work, cleaning and other service areas.

Traffickers, who have built up increasingly sophisticated international networks, offer transport, documents, accommodation, work contacts and help in smoothing the path of entry with the host country authorities. The Washington-based Global Survival Network found that traffickers in Russia and the former Soviet states asked between €1,500 (US$1,500) and €30,000 for a variety of services. These fees, of course, leave women with huge debts.

Exact details depend on the country being supplied. There is some evidence, fieldworkers report, that Russian police can obtain false passports using real information, and that Interpol computer files can be adapted accordingly. With Poles requiring no visa for entry into Germany, fake Polish passports are common for women transiting from Russia and Ukraine. Police complicity has also arisen: in 1996 the chief of Germany's Special Commission on Organised Crime in the Polish border region was charged with controlling a ring of trafficked East European women.

In Belgium, the method of choice is now the asylum request. The overworked system can, according to Anne Vauthier of the victim support group Pag-Asa in Brussels, take between four and eight months to process an asylum claim. During that time the women are put to work in prostitution. When the date for a refusal (the fate of 90% of all claimants) comes, the woman will have been moved on.

In fact, according to figures from the Belgian Centre for Equal Opportunities, a majority of the women who come to the notice of victim support groups are illegal aliens with no papers. Tourist visas were held by 8.5% of women, and asylum-seeker status by 6.5%. At first, the woman may be employed, for example as a waitress in a bar operated by associates of the trafficker. Once the woman is installed, however, she can be forced into prostitution.

For most of the women involved, their stay is ghastly. In general, trafficked women work as lowly street prostitutes. Recently in Brussels, Belgian prostitutes (who carry out their trade from shop-window premises in fairly well-defined city areas) called on police to tackle Albanian and Yugoslav newcomers, who were allegedly undercutting the market and spreading disease by agreeing to sex without condoms. Elsewhere, GSN found, sex in some German clubs employing trafficked women can cost as little as €18. In Brussels, it was alleged, immigrant prostitutes were charging half of the normal market price of €50.

The woman, typically, sees little or none of the money she makes. This is part of the strategy of keeping control over her. And then there is threatened and actual violence. Stories circulate of two Russian prostitutes thrown to their deaths in Istanbul before the eyes of six of their 'colleagues'. A Ukrainian woman who escaped traffickers in Serbia told of her friend who was beheaded. Such tales do little to encourage women to go for help to the authorities.

For a woman unused to western ways and unable to speak the local language, the mere threat of being denounced as an illegal can be enough to keep her in check. 'Trafficked women are kept isolated,' says Joanna Maycock. 'They have no contact with anyone other than clients and each other. In fact, one of the reasons they are moved on after a time is to prevent them establishing firmer links in the country.'

The currents of illegal trafficking flow are exceedingly complex but the Netherlands is a hub for all forms of traffic. The UK tends to be a terminus. Some source countries are also transit and destination countries. According to former UN Special Representative and Coordinator of Operations in Bosnia and Herzegovina Elizabeth Rehn, women from Ukraine, Romania and Moldova work in brothels in Bosnia which may be used by SFOR troops in the region. 'As head of a peacekeeping mission which is 97% male,' she said in Strasbourg in March, 'I cannot turn my back on this subject and I cannot be so naive to think that my staff are not visiting brothels which hold women in slavery.'

Women are also traded among traffickers. According to court papers in a case in Antwerp in 1998, a Russian girl of 20 was taken from home to Germany by her Russian handler to work as a waitress. There, she was sold for €2,500. When stopped for papers by police, she was placed in an asylum-seekers' reception centre, and from there she was taken by two Moldavians to work in Belgium. She was then sold on to a Yugoslav, who severely beat her and threatened to kill her if she went to the police, which nevertheless she eventually did. The man was sentenced to five years in prison. In more recent press reports in Belgium, women trafficked from Ukraine and Bulgaria were being sold between pimps for around €1,000.

More subtle methods of pressure, says Anne Vauthier, can be exercised on the family back home. 'Many of these women may have children. The traffickers usually are on good terms with the families back home, and we've had cases where they took the child off for a day out ... When [the woman] found out about the day out, she knew the power they had.' Threats don't even need to be carried out: the mere possibility of harm to family is enough, she says.

Various international treaties going back to 1904 cover trafficking and there are a variety of initiatives to tackle the problem. The EU has set up STOP (Sexual Trafficking of Persons) for an initial five-year period which ends next year. The budget is small – €1.5 million per year. The thrust of the programme is training staff who work with trafficked women, gathering data and developing action programmes.

The IOM, meanwhile, carries out information campaigns in source countries, using radio and TV campaigns and school visits to push home the essential point that an offer of a good job in the West may seem too good to be true simply because it is. It also carries out research on victim profiles and illegal migration flows, as well as setting up voluntary return and resettlement assistance for trafficking victims.

In the meantime, the IOM is trying to spread information on best practice. The Belgian gendarmerie gives out leaflets produced by the CEO in 19 languages to women in refugee centres who may be victims of trafficking, and the Red Cross does something similar. 'If you want to find a model of how to do everything you can, they're doing it here,' Maycock said. ❏

Alan Hope is a freelance journalist working in Brussels. He writes on crime and justice. His book about the Marc Dutroux case will be published later this year

NATASHA WALTER

The love boat

In Albania's chaotic economy, the traffic in women is a way of life

Although it's Albania's third largest city, nothing much happens in the port of Vlore: there are no factories, no tourism, no cinemas, nowhere to go and nothing to do. Nothing, that is, unless you work in Vlore's one growth industry: trafficking in illegal migrants.

Vlore is just 80km from the coast of Italy and the journey takes only two hours by speedboat. This is where thousands of people set off for their journey to what they hope will be a new life. Every night a series of illegal speedboats whizz across the sea, loaded with their urgent freight of desire.

Most passengers are young men from Albania or the former Soviet Union, who are simply looking for a future. But within this stream of migrants is a growing number of Albanian and other eastern European women who are being trafficked into sex work in the West.

Trafficking in women is not a victimless crime. Even those women who agree to go to the West as prostitutes often find that once they arrive in London, or Rome, or Antwerp, or Berlin, they are forced into a sexual slavery that they would never have consented to. 'They are forced to hand over all their earnings,' explains Inspector Paul Holmes of the London vice squad, who is seeing more and more prostitutes under the thumb of the Albanian mafia. 'They are not allowed any choice about the number of clients or the type of sexual services they must offer; and if they resist they or their families at home may be threatened with violence.'

The extent of the problem becomes clearer in Albania. There, you can see how deeply the business of trafficking is embedded into its chaotic economy, and how difficult it is for any individual or organisation to take on the trafficking mafia.

On the Vlore coast I met two of the speedboat drivers, or *scafisti*. 'Seventy per cent of the men in Vlore do this work,' one told me. 'It's the only work I've ever done. I've been doing it for six years. All my family lives on my income. More than 20 people live on the income from one speedboat. How would those people live if we didn't drive the boats?'

I also met Vera Lesko, who is working almost single-handedly against the Albanian mafia in the port. Last year she started to research trafficking for a local women's group. One day she learnt of a girl who had been tricked into an engagement with a trafficker and was being held in a house on the outskirts of Vlore before being taken to work the streets of Rome.

Vera Lesko spoke to the girl. 'She was only 16. I tried to tell her what was waiting for her in the West but she couldn't, or didn't want to, understand me. It was beyond her comprehension, the idea that her new fiancé might want to hurt her.'

Desperate and frustrated, Vera went to the police. She spent several hours trying to persuade them to act but was told there was nothing they could do. Then, on her way home, a man came up to her. 'I'm warning you,' he said. 'If you try this again your own daughter will be next. And you won't live to see her come back.' Terrified, Vera ran the few blocks to her home, to find every window in her apartment smashed.

Her daughter has now left town, but Vera goes on working. If she can get the necessary funding her organisation, the Centre for the Development of Vlore Women will set up a refuge for trafficked women. 'I am afraid,' she says softly. 'But what else can I do? These women could be my daughter.' ❏

Natasha Walter *is a columnist with the* Independent

BOB SUTCLIFFE

To borrow and to borrow

Debt bondage doesn't affect only individuals and families: it has shackled entire nations

If slavery is a state of having others take all-important decisions about your life, owing obligations to others with no hope that you can ever pay them off, working for others without fair recompense and with no end in sight, being in danger of severe punishment if you try to escape and suffering a prohibition against organising with other people with similar problems, then the external debt of poor countries today is a form of slavery.

Behind what is formally a financial obligation, voluntarily entered into, lies a burdensome system of economic payments which involves a cynical connivance in the suppression of human rights. The present external debt of developing countries debt is illegitimate, in most senses of the word: it is a literally insupportable economic burden; it was entered into with assurances from the lenders, which turned out to be false; it was incurred by one group of people, who often gained from it, but it is being paid by another, which had no part in the decision and now suffers directly from it.

Much of the debt is recognised as unpayable. The big debtors – Argentina, Mexico, Brazil, Russia, China, Indonesia and South Korea – owe between US$100 billion and US$200 billion each. But, relative to the size of their economies, these debts are still small when compared with the poorer debtors in Africa. The total of what they owe is peanuts in international terms but, in at least 11 cases, despite some debt reduction in recent years, total debt still amounts to more than two years of the sum of all national economic activity, exportable or otherwise.

The tiny republic of São Tomé e Príncipe heads this lamentable list at present by owing over six years of all it produces. Others, which owe more than two years of their national income, are Guinea-Bissau, Nicaragua, Angola, Congo-Brazzaville, Mozambique, Mauritania, Democratic Republic of Congo, Guyana, Sudan and Zambia. Hence the poorest countries of the world are, as a rule, also the most indebted. The German reparations debt, which John Maynard Keynes in 1919 famously (in *The Economic Consequences of the Peace*) denounced as oppressive, unpayable and the source of future turmoil, amounted to only three years of the German national income.

The most debt-burdened countries do not, of course, pay all they owe. Arrears on interest are currently calculated as about US$35 billion, mostly owed by poor countries in Africa. Nevertheless, the most indebted actually pay what for them are vast amounts. In 1997, 16 countries paid in debt service (interest and repayments) more than 30% of their total export earnings. These included both very poor and not so poor countries. According to the World Bank's preliminary estimates, Sub-Saharan African countries in 1998 paid a total of over US$14 billion in debt service and received about US$10 billion in development aid (excluding technical assistance). In this sense the poorest countries actually send economic aid to the rich ones.

Keynes also pointed out that Germany in 1919 was not only forced to be a debtor but was also prevented by the victorious allies from expanding its exports – the only way in which the debt could be paid. Again the parallel with many of today's poorest African countries is close, which partly explains their present anger with a world trading system in which they have seen their share of world exports fall from over 3% of the world total in 1950, when they were still colonies, to around 1% today.

About 60% of the developing countries' current total of US$2000 billion of debt is owed to banks and bondholders; about 25% to states in bilateral obligations and the remaining 15% to multilateral bodies (the IMF, the World Bank, regional development banks and the European Union). These shares are very different between regions. Africa owes almost entirely to bilateral and multilateral public creditors, while Latin America and East Asia owe the bulk of their debt to private creditors. While banks sometimes have to accept delays in payment, and even on occasions are forced to write off bad debts, none of these private credits is considered in current plans for debt forgiveness.

This should make the situation easier for poor African countries which owe public creditors, but it doesn't. The World Bank is the most difficult creditor of all in the sense that its loans come with the proviso that they must be the first to be paid. But the official bilateral creditors, which do not expect the debts to be paid and whose finances would not be dented by non-payment, are extremely parsimonious when it comes to debt forgiveness, mostly because they can continue to employ the debt relationship as a neo-colonial political lever. What little unpayable debt they have forgiven, they then cynically add to their dwindling development aid figures as if it were a form of new payment.

The debt-forgiveness initiatives which have so far come from the IMF, World Bank and leading creditor nations are extremely partial and timid. They are all based on the premise that the debt is legitimate, but that it may be partially forgiven on condition that the indebted countries give proof over a number of years that they will introduce good economic government. Such conditionality, characteristic of all North-South economic relations, is both imperialist and self-defeating. The very existence of the debt, and the pressures which it creates, helps to lead both to bad economic government and to undemocratic politics.

Campaigns against the debt often point out that the governments of developing countries spend nearly three times as much on external debt service as they do on public health. Of course, this does not mean that, if the debt were cancelled, the money saved would automatically be spent on public welfare. It would be spent on the priorities of the governments, which may well not be socially useful. But the debt makes it easier for reactionary governments to blame foreign creditors for their own bad intentions. And when bad governments are replaced by more democratic and better-intentioned ones, the debt makes life very much harder: the first headache in office is always how to manage and pay off the debts of former dictators, rather than how to meet the backlog of needs of their own peoples.

So, to call the consequences of the developing countries' external debt a form of slavery is a good deal more than a metaphor. ❏

Bob Sutcliffe *is an economist specialising in development and immigration, who teaches at the University of the Basque Country in Bilbao*

Defining terror

We are a terribly forgetful lot here in the UK. We introduced our drink licensing laws as a temporary measure in WWI to stop hungover munitions workers putting a widget where the oozalum should go – and here we are still soberly jettisoned from pubs at 11.15pm because someone forgot to repeal the law. We lent a few hundred acres of moorland to the US in WWII so they could practice their electronic eavesdropping on our subversive heather, and stone me if 50 years later we've gone and forgotten to kick them out.

Lucky for us that in 1974 the Prevention of Terrorism Act was purpose-built as a temporary measure, designed to be renewed a year at a time. No excuses then, for forgetting what a repressive piece of law it was. As the decades ticked by the role call of those falsely arrested, exiled and jailed continued to trouble those of liberal conscience. The Labour opposition withdrew support for the Act, and by doing so drew fire annually in those long years of Conservative rule. But they were also long years of conflict in Northern Ireland and on the British mainland. On balance the Act was seen as necessary, even if those who enforced it were known to be overzealous. After all, once a solution was found to the turmoil in Northern Ireland, the arbitrary arrests, lengthy detention without access to a lawyer and internal exile would all come to an end. We thought.

Despite bitterness and bloody-mindedness, things are changing in Northern Ireland – the IRA ceasefire is, militarily, rock solid, and has been for two years. The squaddies may not yet be confined to barracks, but kevlar helmets have been replaced by regimental berets. Peace is no longer an impossible dream.

What is Home Secretary Jack Straw's response? To take the most repressive aspects of the Prevention of Terrorism Act (POTA), add a range of anti-democratic restrictions, blend in a dash of extra-territorial legislation and make the Act permanent. To focus outrage on the break this makes with previous Labour arguments is pointless – New Labour has disavowed so many shibboleths of old that even Keir Hardie must have stopped spinning in his grave by now. Beyond party politics, there are instead two issues of absolute importance.

The first is that a raft of extreme measures, originally designed to target an emergency situation, is to be reinforced and made permanent despite the ending of that specific emergency. The UK has cited the Northern Ireland emergency several times before the European Court of Human Rights, to explain the persistent breaches of human rights that the POTA has contributed to. Is the government now suggesting the emergency has become perpetual? Once the IRA cuts up its rifles and flushes away its Semtex, who is threatening our society? If we are forever abandoning certain democratic rights, could Jack Straw reveal which new enemy has forced this on us? The Zapatistas? Sendero Luminoso? Or might it be, perhaps, Greenpeace? Nice trick Jack – when you run out of terrorists, hey, just change the definition of terrorism...

That's the second, shocking, departure made by the Terrorism Bill from previous practice. In the 1974 Act terrorism was defined as 'the use of violence for political ends [including] any use of violence for the purpose of putting the public, or any section of the public in fear'. Few would argue with that. In 1999's Bill terrorism had become 'the use of serious violence against persons or property, or the threat to use such violence, to intimidate or coerce a government, the public or any section of the public for political, religious or ideological ends.' The extension of the definition to include religious and ideological ends is not, in most eyes, contentious. It is the references to property and threats that first create unease, and, crucially, it is the definition of 'serious violence' included elsewhere in the Bill that marks this out as the work of an authoritarian mind – does creating 'serious disruption' for the community strike you as the equivalent of doing 'serious violence' to that community?

Any major street demonstration creates disruption – often that is the goal. Extra-parliamentary actions are not just the preserve of mad bombers. From the suffragettes to anti-WTO activists by way of CND and poll tax *refusniks*, street protestors and direct actioners have had a powerful and generally positive effect on society. As Lord Justice Hoffman said in reference to the Twyford Down environmental protestors: 'Civil disobedience on grounds of conscience is an honourable tradition in this country and those who take part in it may in the end be vindicated by history.' Under this Bill anyone blocking a road, occupying buildings, even hacking a website would run the risk of being labelled a terrorist – and would suffer additional punishments as such. Their organisations, if any, would be defined as terrorist, and proscribed. Membership or support of proscribed organisations would be punishable by 10 years in jail.

Jack Straw protests that this legislation will not be used against 'legitimate' pressure groups – yet the capacity is clearly there, and who knows what a future government will consider legitimate or not? This is a dangerous, ill-timed, disproportionate piece of law. In function it further disempower's the ordinary citizen faced with a growing democratic deficit in Westminster, Brussels and, as we saw in Seattle, wherever the peripatetic WTO makes its home.

In large part, popular rights in the UK have been won by popular, not executive, action. Throughout the last millennium when the executive has introduced universal suffrage, jury trials, the rights to assembly and association, it has done so under pressure – often after 'serious disruption', and worse. As we approach the next millennium, let's not forget what we spent most of this one fighting for. ❏

Frank Fisher

A censorship chronicle incorporating information from the American Association for the Advancement of Science Human Rights Action Network (AAASHRAN), Amnesty International (AI), Article 19 (A19), the BBC Monitoring Service Summary of World Broadcasts (SWB), the Committee to Protect Journalists (CPJ), Canadian Journalists for Free Expression (CJFE), Glasnost Defence Foundation (GDF), Instituto de Prensa y Sociedad (IPYS), The UN's Integrated Regional Information Network (IRIN), the Inter-American Press Association (IAPA), the International Federation of Journalists (IFJ/FIP), Human Rights Watch (HRW), the Media Institute of Southern Africa (MISA), Network for the Defence of Independent Media in Africa (NDIMA), International PEN (PEN), Open Media Research Institute (OMRI), Pacific Islands News Association (PINA), Radio Free Europe/Radio Liberty (RFE/RL), Reporters Sans Frontières (RSF), the World Association of Community Broadcasters (AMARC), World Association of Newspapers (WAN), the World Organisation Against Torture (OMCT) and other sources

ALGERIA

On 10 November **Omar Belhouchet**, publisher of the daily *El Watan,* was sentenced to one year imprisonment for accusing the government regime of involvement in the assassination of journalists. (*Algeria Interface*)

ANGOLA

Journalist and human rights activist **Rafael Marques**, who was arrested in Luanda by security officers (DNIC) on 16 October (*Index* 6/1999), was granted bail on 25 November, well after the 15-day limitation on detention without trial. He remained under house arrest. (HRW, MISA)

After threatening independent media which did not support the war against UNITA (*Index* 5/1999), Information Minister Hendrik Vaal Neto announced, on 5 November a review of the Press Law. The journalists union broadly welcomed the move and the new opportunity for dialogue with the government. (MISA)

ARGENTINA

Media organisations and trade unions expressed disapproval at the announcement of a bill on 1 September intended to regulate radio and television announcers. If passed, the bill would assign to announcers, duties normally carried out by journalists. (*Periodistas*)

Following a hearing at the Inter American Commission of Human Rights on 1 October, the new government accepted *Periodistas'* demand for increased press freedoms. In January the organisation filed complaints against three rulings of the Supreme Court (*Index* 5/1999), and questioned a further 12 sentences that curtailed citizens' right to receive information. President Fernando de la Rua promised to consider a bill which would

include laws to safeguard journalists and a free press. (*Periodistas*, Freedom Forum).

Journalist **Daniel Tognetti** from the television programme *Caiga Quien Caiga* was assaulted on 17 October, following a gathering of the Partido Justicialista. Tognetti, who required hospital treatment, was attacked by the occupants of a vehicle identified as as belonging to the organisers of the event. (*Periodistas*)

On 10 November a warrant was issued for the arrest of six people connected with the assassination of journalist **Ricardo Gangeme** (*Index* 4/1999). The journalist, who had been investigating the director of the Trelew Electrical Cooperative, was assassinated five days after receiving death threats. (*Periodistas*)

While driving in the capital on 13 November, radio journalist **Mario Otero** was intimidated by two police officers. Two days later, the officers were suspended from duty and an internal inquiry was launched to investigate the incident. Otero had been working on irregularities arising from the reappearance of a certain Claudia Diez five years after police had concluded that she died while having an abortion. (*Periodistas*)

The preliminary hearing of the trial investigating the assassination of the photographer **José Luís Cabezas** started on 15 November. To avoid any further delay, judges decided to limit the number of witnesses to 300. The newspaper *Página 12*, suggested that the defence strategy is to prevent any verdict being delivered before April 2000, at which point the accused would have to be freed in accordance with the law which permits detainees held in custody for over three years to escape sentence. (*Periodistas*)

On 17 November Ramon Diaz, technical manager of the soccer team Club Atletico River Plate, filed a defamation suit against journalist **Adrián Paenza** following his accusation that Diaz had demanded money from players in order to keep their places in the team. Soccer's national governing body, the Fair Play Foundation, also accused Diaz of extortion and coercion in the Preliminary Court. (*Perioditas*)

ARMENIA

On 11 November the new prime minister, Aram Sargisian, rejected calls for curbs on the press or freedom of speech as the government struggled to restore political stability. Sargisian was making his first public speech since his appointment to replace his brother Vazgen, assassinated during an attack during a parliamentary debate on 27 October. (RFE/RL)

AUSTRALIA

During a Senate debate on the government's controversial Internet censorship bill on 30 September, Minister for Communications, Information Technology and the Arts

Richard Alston described the critical organisation Electronic Frontiers Australia as 'maniacs' who are 'not in the slightest bit interested in the welfare of the community'. He went on to accuse them of causing problems between the Internet Industry Association and the government, which have dogged the negotiation of a code of practice. (Electronic Frontiers Australia)

AZERBAIJAN

Thirty-four employees of independent TV company Sara began an indefinite hunger strike on 19 October in protest at a 250 million manat ($US62,000) fine imposed on the company for 'insulting the honour and dignity of a government official' (*Index* 6/1999). On 1 November, 14 employees were continuing the protest, three of whom had been hospitalised. Meanwhile, Sara TV lawyers are appealing against the Justice Ministry decision to close the station because it is allegedly foreign-owned. (RFE/RL)

Recent publications: *Comments on the Initial Report Submitted to the United Nations Committee Against Torture* (AI, October 1999, 45pp)

BANGLADESH

On 21 October **Amran Hussain** of the *Daily Star*, **Rafiqur Rahman** of Reuters Photo and **Khalid Haider** of *Dainik Dinkal* were injured by a bomb thrown at them while they were covering an opposition Bangladesh National Party demonstration.

The following day, several journalists were beaten by police in Dhaka after they filmed officers attacking Islamic activists. (RSF, CPJ)

On 1 November **Sanual Huq** and **Anisur Rahman**, photographers for *The Independent* and *Daily Star* newspapers respectively, were seriously injured after police fired at them during a protest of opposition parties. Both journalists remain in intensive care. Later that day, two vehicles owned by the newspapers *Dainik Ajker Kagoj* and *Bhorer Kagoj* were damaged by opposition activists who also threatened the journalists inside. (RSF)

Press photographer **Mahe Alam James** was shot on 8 November by police firing at an alliance of opposition party demonstrators in Dhaka. The incident took place on the second day of of a country-wide general strike. (RSF)

BELARUS

On 6 October the independent weekly *Balaruskala Maladzyozhnaya* was threatened with closure by the State Press Committee. The threat came at the request of Minsk tax inspectors who claimed the publication violated press law as its editorial office was not located at the paper's officially registered address. In a private conversation with a tax inspector, chief editor **Tatsyana Malnichuk** was informed of 'an instruction from the top' to close down the paper. (RFE/RL)

On 1 November Mikail Chyhir, the former premier charged with organising mass demonstrations, was told he would have to wait another month for a trial date. Chyhir also stands accused of abuses of power and 'criminal negligence'. (RFE/RL)

On 4 November President Alexandr Lukashenka overturned a protocol granting the Social Democratic Party access to the state-controlled media, despite its approval by his representatives. Intended to permit the SDP to show pre-recorded videos on state television, Lukashenka claimed the protocol would have contravened 'all civilised and democratic norms' by enabling the party to introduce 'its own censorship' into the state media, while also depriving journalists of their authorship rights. (RFE/RL)

Alek Byalatski, leader of the Human Rights Organisation Spring-96, was arrested on 18 November. Called to Minsk district police department to collect computers that had been confiscated from his organisation in early October, he was arrested as one of the planners of the 17 October Freedom March. (RFE/RL)

BOSNIA-HERZEGOVINA

On 3 November television journalist **Srdoje Srdic** was attacked by the mayor of Doboj, Mivko Stojcinvic, following the broadcast of a report on local corruption. After the assault, the mayor told Srdic to leave Doboj or he would 'liquidate' him. (RSF)

On 10 November **Andjelko Kozomara**, the head of radio and television in the Republika Srpska, was reportedly sacked by Prime Minister Milorad Dodik and replaced by Slavisa Sabljic. Parliament is to discuss the controversial rearrangement as Dodik claimed Kozomara was removed 'because he had become too close to President Milosevic'. (RFE/RL)

On 16 November the Independent Media Commission ordered Erotel TV, a private station serving the Croatian community, to stop broadcasting. Based in Mostar, Erotel TV had been operating without a licence for two years, retransmitting programmes from state-run Croatian television. (RFE/RL)

BURKINA FASO

In the last week of November a series of demonstrations marked the first anniversary of the brutal murder of the former editor in chief of the weekly *l'Independantt*, **Norbert Zongo,** and three of his friends (*Index* 2/1999, 5/1999, 6/1999). Prior to his death he had been investigating the death in custody of David Ouedraogo, an employee of the president's brother. A general strike was planned for 13 December, to commemorate their deaths. (RSF)

On 1 December **Paulin Yameogo**, director of the opposition-linked weekly *San Finna*, was arrested and taken to the National Security headquarters in Ouagadougou.

He is accused of publishing a photograph of **Ilboudo Hamidou**, bearing marks of torture, after his arrest by presidential guard soldiers in December 1997. Hamidou was detained at the same time as David Ouedraogo, the chauffeur of President Blaise Compaoré's brother, who was tortured to death in January 1998. (RSF)

On the same day **Boureima Sigue**, director of the private daily *Le Pays*, was arrested and released some hours later, following the publication of an opposition text calling for guarantees to 'the security of all protesters' and an end to 'the terrorist methods used by the minority who cling to power'. (RSF)

BURMA

Democracy activist **Rachel Goldwyn** arrived in England on 8 November following her release from Rangoon's Insein prison one week earlier(*Index* 6/1999). After 'quiet negotiations' between the British Embassy and the authorities, the 28-year-old was released after serving six weeks of a seven-year sentence for singing a pro-democracy song. Goldwyn, who signed an agreement not to become involved in Burmese political activities again, vowed to 'pursue dialogue' as opposed to confrontation in the future. Fellow British activist **James Mawdsley**, sentenced to 17 years' imprisonment (*Index* 6/1999), will not be freed early as he had broken a promise not to return to the country. (Associated Press)

American **Dan Sadler** was deported from Cambodia on 5 November, two weeks after his arrest for 'operating an Internet pornography site'. He was arrested after Minister for Women's Affairs Mu Sochua complained about an article published in the daily *Cambodia*, in which Sadler stated that he had used pictures of ethnic Vietnamese rather than local women to 'avoid angering the government'. (Reuters)

CHECHNYA

Freelance photojournalist **Brice Fleutiaux** disappeared around 1 October. On 31 October Russia's FSB security services broadcast footage of an unshaven man standing in a dark room complaining in French about poor treatment by his captors. A FSB spokesman claimed that Chechen kidnappers had made the tape and given it to them in order to collect ransom for Fleutiaux's release. (CPJ)

On 8 October journalists Anthony Lloyd of *the Times* and Tyler Hicks of the *New York Times* were detained at the border from Ingushetia for lacking documents. They were attempting to enter the state with an Islamic peacemaking group which was also refused entry. (GDF)

On 25 October Radio Liberty correspondent **Oleg Kusov** was deprived of his dictaphone by a Russian officer near the border with Ingushetia. On asking for an explanation, Kusov was hit by the officer with the butt of his rifle.

(GDF)

Supian Ependiyev, a journalist on the independent weekly *Groznenskiy Rabochiy*, died on 29 October. Ependiyev was wounded two days earlier by a rocket attack while reporting on an earlier, similar incident in the middle of Grozny. On the same day, cameraman **Ramzan Mezhidov**, of Moscow's TV Tsentr, and **Shamil Yegayev** of the independent, Grozny-based Nokh Cho television were also killed while filming a Russian air attack on a refugee convoy. They were the first journalists to be killed in Russia's second military campaign in the breakaway republic. (CPJ, GDF)

CHINA

On 1 October **Xu Wenli**, a founder of the outlawed Democracy Party currently serving a 13-year sentence (*Index* 2/1999, 5/1999), was given a four-hour car 'tour' of the capital to enlighten him as to the transformation of Beijing during the 50 years of communist rule. Having contracted a form of hepatitis while in prison and being denied the necessary medical care, he was unable to open his eyes. (Associated Press)

Wu Yilong, **Zhu Yufu**, **Mao Qingxiang** and **Xu Guang**, all affiliated with the banned China Democratic Party, were sentenced to between five and 11 years' imprisonment on 25 October, for 'subverting state power' by establishing an Internet magazine. (Agence France-Presse)

Having already accused the Falun Gong movement (*Index* 5/1999, 6/1999) of responsibility for 1,400 deaths, the destruction of the 'normal social order', illegal gatherings, rape and theft, the government introduced new legislation on 30 October which allows judicial authorities to retrospectively prosecute members active before the 22 July ban, and charge the cult's leaders with murder and endangering national security – offences that carry the death penalty. Fearing a new crackdown, small groups of practitioners travelled to Beijing to stage peaceful demonstrations in the last week of October. Over 4,000 protestors, many of them middle-aged women, are believed to have been temporarily detained and 'educated' about the evils of the movement. On 12 November the first known trial involving 111 Falun Gong members began. Charged with 'using an evil cult to violate the law', **Song Yueshang** was sentenced to 12 years' imprisonment. Despite government assurances that only leaders of the movement would be prosecuted, human rights activists claimed that 300 people are awaiting trial, while another 2,000 are expected to attend 'education through labour' camps – a punishment that does not require a trial. Also in October police arrested **Zhang Ji**, a student at Qiqihar University in Heilongjiang province, and **Li Fujun**, a medical college instructor in Henan, and charged them with 'using the Internet to spread

XINHUA NEWS AGENCY
The people's press

Investigation has found that the Qinghai People's Publishing House published four books advocating the Falun Gong cult. These books were circulated after pirating by illegal book firms. ...

The actions of the publishing house severely violated the pertinent state legislation on publishing. The Press and Publications Office issued a circular to shut down the publishing house for rectification, circulating the criticism to the publishing world throughout China. The Press and Publications Office demands that the Qinghai People's Publishing House must completely clear up its problems in editing, publishing, distributing and operating management, as well as confiscating and destroying Falun Gong books. The Qinghai Party Committee and government ... have decided to reorganise the leadership of both the Qinghai Press and Publications Office and the Qinghai People's Publishing House, punishing the major officials by dismissing them and through severe inner-Party warnings and demotions.

In 1996, the Press and Publications Office issued a circular, clearly banning the publication of Falun Gong books that advocate ignorant superstition and pseudo-science, stipulating the corresponding administrative sanctions for publishing units involved in publishing such books. The Qinghai People's Publishing House ignored the ban. This severely violated the publishing direction of serving the people and socialism, was out of line with the building of a socialist spiritual civilisation and was a severe case with an evil effect.

A Press and Publications Office official stresses that publishing circles need to learn a lesson from the mistakes of the Qinghai People's Publishing House, adhering to the correct publishing orientation, abiding strictly by publishing legislation and always giving first place to the social effect ... by publishing more and better outstanding publications for the masses. ❏

Edited version of a report published by Xinhua, the official Chinese news agency, on 29 November. Falun Gong was outlawed by the ministry of civil affairs on 22 July.

subversive information' about the Falun Gong. Three days later the Foreign Correspondents' Club protested after five journalists were detained for attending a clandestine Falun Gong press conference. The journalists, from agencies including Reuters, the *New York Times* and Associated Press, had their work and residency papers temporarily confiscated. In defence of the action, a spokeswoman asked foreign journalists to observe the rule of law by not covering the illegal organisation.

The Falun Gong hoped to use the visit of UN Secretary General Kofi Annan to demand an official inquiry into the government's treatment of the group. On his arrival on 16 November, 15 members were detained in Tiananmen Square as they unfurled a red banner and began their calisthenic exercises. Although his access to them was restricted, Annan professed in a press conference to having a 'better understanding' of the crackdown after talks with Foreign Minister Tang Jiaxuan in which he was assured of the government's respect for the 'fundamental rights' of the movement's practitioners. Nonetheless, human rights groups claim that at least six members of the movement have died in police custody since August. These include the 18-year-old student **Chen Ying**, who died under police escort when she jumped from the bathroom window of a train, and **Zhao Jinghua**, who was beaten to death. Police acknowledge these deaths, but

they deny any involvement. The new legislation of 30 October also signalled a wider crackdown against other unsanctioned religious organisations. The founder of the Guo (National) Gong sect, **Liu Jineng** and aides **Liu Jun** and **Deng Guoquan**, were arrested soon afterwards while on 2 November **Xiao Yun**, the guru of the Cibei (Compassion) Gong group, was also arrested and charged with earning illegal profits and having illicit sexual relations with four women. Most dramatically, **Liu Jiaguo**, the leader of a popular group called Principal God, in Hunan province, was executed having been convicted of raping 11 women. (Agence France-Presse, *Washington Post*)

On 25 November authorities arrested four foreign supporters of the banned spiritual movement in the southern Chinese city of Guangzhou. **Sun Jie**, a Chinese-American, **Anne Hakosalo**, a Swedish exchange student, **Jiang Huijie** and **Jiang Xili**, two Australian-Chinese, were detained at a gathering in the city. They were released shortly afterwards. Meanwhile, a leaked speech by Politburo Standing Committee member Li Lanqing on 26 November enabled the Hong Kong-based Information Center of Human Rights & Democratic Movement in China (ICHRDM) to claim that 35,792 members had been detained between 20 July and 30 October. (Agence France-Presse, Reuters, *Washington Post*, *New York Times*, *Guardian*, Associated Press, AI)

Hundreds of Tibetans took to the streets in protest in the Kandze Tibetan Autonomous Prefecture (TAP), Sichuan province in early November after the arrest of a respected Buddhist teacher and two other monks. The arrests may have been linked to the bombing of a small Tibetan medical clinic in a nearby village in October. At least 300 people are said to have been involved in what amounts to one of the largest protests in Tibetan areas since the late 1980s. Armed troops reportedly used tear gas and guns to break up the demonstration and at least 50 Tibetans were detained. (TIN)

It was reported on 10 November that **Mehmet Adullah Sidhi** and 17 other Muslim separatists from Xinjiang Autonomous Region were sentenced to between one and 15 years' imprisonment for spreading 'splittist theories' and 'undermining the unity of the motherland'. They were also convicted of organising assemblies, recruiting members and gathering 'reactionary' books and magazines. (Agence France-Presse)

Dissident **Wang Wanxing**, who was held for more than seven years after he unfurled a protest banner in Tiananmen square in 1992, was 'readmitted' to Ankang psychiatric hospital on 23 November. The hospital is run by the Public Security Bureau for those deemed 'criminally insane'. It is believed he was forcibly returned after he declared his intention to hold a news conference describing his experiences. (*New York Times, Human Rights in China*)

An Jun, an independent anti-corruption activist, was tried on 24 November for 'inciting the overthrow of state political power' and general activities threatening social stability. In 1998, An Jun organised the China Corrupt Behavioral Observer, with a membership of some 300 people in 12 provinces, which uncovered over 100 cases of corruption. (Agence France-Presse)

Recent Publications: *Not Welcome at the Party: Behind the 'Clean-Up' of China's Cities – A Report on Administrative Detention Under 'Custody and Repatriation'*, Human Rights in China, September 1999; *People's Republic of China, Reports of Torture and Ill Treatment of Followers of the Falun Gong*, AI October 1999.

COLOMBIA

On 21 October **Rodolfo Julio Torres**, Fuentes local radio station correspondent in Cartagena, was shot in the head three times after he was kidnapped from his home by four men. (Associated Press)

Seven journalists were abducted on 29 October by the members of the Revolutionary Armed Forces (FARC) after leaving the oil-refining town of Barrancabermeja by boat. At the invitation of the FARC, the reporters had been heading to the southern Bolivar department to cover the displacement of local farmers

by paramilitary forces. The guerrillas contacted the Bucaramanga daily *Vanguardia Libera*, where one of the hostages worked, to say that the journalists would not be released until they 'reported the truth' about atrocities committed against local farmers. They were all released three days later. (CPJ)

Seven journalists were kidnapped on 10 November while travelling to cover a paramilitary attack in Atanquez. So far, no group has claimed responsibiilty for the abductions. (CPJ)

A bomb exploded at a bus stop near the offices of the local daily *El Tiempo* on 14 November, injuring three employees. Responsibility for the attack was claimed by several organisations, including the FARC, the National Liberation Army and the Patriotic Resistance. (RSF)

On 23 November journalist **María Cristina Caballero** received the 1999 CPJ International Press Freedom Award. As a reporter for the magazine *Semana*, she has been frequently threatened for her coverage of the war. (CPJ)

On 28 November cameraman **Luís Alberto Rincón** and reporter **Alberto Sánchez** were shot dead while covering local elections to replace the mayor of El Playon, who was himself assassinated by gunmen in September. The journalists, who both worked for local television stations, were were found dead at the roadside near the town. (RSF)

CHILE

On 1 October, US Immigration gave political asylum to **Alejandra Matus** (*Index* 5/1999), the Chilean journalist who fled to Miami following the April banning of her publication *The Black Book of the Chilean Justice*, which chronicled abuses of power by the Supreme Court during General Augusto Pinochet's military regime (1973-90). (Derechos)

COTE D'IVOIRE

On 20 October **Raphael Lapke** and **Jean Khalil Sylla** (*Index* 4/99), publisher and editor of the daily *Le Populaire*, were sentenced to six months' imprisonment following their conviction for distributing and disclosing false news. Their arrest followed the publication of an article by Sylla on 28 April, which wrongly reported police officers as having killed a student. On 29 October, Raphael Lapke was released after serving his sentence. Sylla was expected to remain in prison until 10 December. (CPJ, RSF)

On 25 October the offices of the daily *Libération* were looted and the night-watchman killed. This follows the murder of *Libération*'s former owner **Abdoulaye Bakayoko** (*Index* 6/199) on 21 September and a reported assassination attempt against the paper's manager **Lana Fofama** six days later. (RSF)

CUBA

On 10 November authorities

in Santiago detained **Santiago Santana**, director of the Eastern Free Press Agency, and confiscated his ticket to Havana where he intended to cover the Ibero-America summit. Since the beginning of November, approximately 100 people have been allegedly detained or placed under house arrest in relation to the summit. Immediately prior to the summit, RSF appealed for the release of journalists **Bernardo Arévalo Padrón, Manuel Antonio González Castellanos, Leonardo Varona González** and **Jesús Joel Díaz Hernández**, who have each been sentenced to between six years and 16 months in jail for 'insulting' the head of state. (RSF)

Angel Pablo Polanco of the Independent Journalists Cooperative (IJC) and **Omar Rodriguez** of the New Press Agency were arrested in Havana on 10 November while preparing to cover a demonstration by human rights organisations. (RSF)

Journalist **Jesús Joel Díaz Hernández** received the CPI International Press Freedom Award for 1999 on 23 November. He is currently serving a four-year sentence for launching an independent news agency critical of the government. (CPJ)

DEMOCRATIC REPUBLIC OF CONGO

One year since his arrest (*Index* 2/1999), **Joseph Mbakulu Pambu Diana** continues to be detained without trial. He is currently held in solitary confinement in Kinshasa prison. (RSF)

Polycarpe Honsek Okwoy, director of the weekly *La Solidarité*, has been detained in solitary confinement since 6 November. She is accused of publishing an article which falsely refers to the arrest of the minister of finance. (RSF)

Feu d'Or Bonsange and **Kala Bongamba**, employees of the newspaper *L'Alarme*, were released without charge on 29 September two days after their arrest. **Clovis Kadda**, another employee of *L'Alarme*, is in hiding following his arrest and torture at the Kinshasa military headquarters on 22 September. (WiPC)

On 7 November **Djodo Kazadi**, director of the Kinshasa weekly *La Palme d'Or*, was arrested at home without explanation by an armed, unidentified man. In a recent editon, *La Palme d'Or* had published an article alleging that the inhabitants of Kivu, a rebel-controlled region, wanted to bring Laurent-Desire Kabila before the courts. (RSF)

DJIBOUTI

Journalist **Eric Monier** and cameraman **Roger Motte**, of the television station France 2, were expelled on 22 October for having sought to 'tarnish the image' of the country and harm 'relations between the government and France'. (RSF)

EGYPT

On 10 October, the Court of Cessation upheld an earlier ruling to remove a freeze on the activities of a lawyers' syndicate, sanctioned three years ago. Nonetheless, there was scepticism as to whether the syndicate would be able to hold elections for a new board prior to the ministry of justice appointing a temporary committee. (*Cairo Times*)

On 16 October the government rounded up 20 prominent members of the banned Muslim Brotherhood after they planned a strategy meeting for upcoming elections to the lawyers' syndicate. They were referred for trial in a military court on 27 October. (*Cairo Times*)

On 7 November a Cairo administrative court upheld a lower court decision to ban the entry of Saudi mystic **Sheikh Shmseddin Al Fasi**, to the country. The ban stemmed from London-based Fasi's claim that Sufi groups performed religiously invalid rituals. (*Cairo Times*)

EIRE

The Idiots, a controversial film by Oscar-nominated writer **Lars Von Trier**, was banned by censor Seamus Smith on 26 October. Smith decided that the film, which includes scenes of nudity including a semi-erect penis, was likely to 'deprave or corrupt viewers'. Film distributors Metro Tartan are considering an appeal. (*Guardian*)

EUROPEAN UNION

On 21 October it was decided that all food containing less than 1% of genetically modified produce will be regarded as 'GM Free' under new labelling rules. Campaigners had pushed for a 'zero tolerance level' for GM-free foods throughout the region. (*Daily Telegraph*)

FIJI

Three *Fiji Times* journalists, **Netani Rika**, **Margaret Wise** and **Matelita Ragogohave**, began defamation proceedings against government MP Muthu Swamy. The action was prompted by a letter to the editor from the MP in which he claimed Wise and another *Fiji Times* journalist, **Josefa Makaba**, had slept together; accused Rika of embezzlement; and stated that Wise and Ragogo had been arrested for drunk and disorderly behaviour. He originally made the claims in the House of Representatives on 24 October, where he presumed that he was protected by parliamentary privilege. (PINA)

It was reported on 25 November that the application to renew the work permit of the Scottish editor-in-chief of the *Fiji Times*, **Russell Hunter**, had been turned down by the government. The rejection was received on the same day that the newspaper accused the government of running a vendetta against it. (PINA)

On 26 October Prime Minister Mahendra Chaudry threatened to introduce a government-controlled authority with powers to impose penalties on the media if it continued to ignore the Public Order Act. Chaudry singled out the biggest daily newspaper, the *Fiji Times*, and the largest television service, Fiji Television, for special criticism, claiming that their journalists possessed a hidden 'agenda'. He also accused the *Fiji Times* of publishing 'anti-government stories with manipulated and distorted facts, designed to discredit and embarrass the government'. The *Daily Post* newspaper, in which the government is the main shareholder, was praised for its work. (PINA)

FINLAND

Amnesty International recently adopted six conscientious objectors, who refused to carry out alternative civilian service because of its punitive length. The new military service law, that came into force in 1998, allows those those who do not wish to undertake 180 days of military service to carry out 395 days of civilian service. The six objectors were each given 197 days' imprisonment for 'non-military service crime'. (AI)

FRANCE

The visit by Mohammed Khatami on 27 October, the first by an Iranian President since the 1979 revolution, was met by human rights protests. Police security was more aggressive than for the visit of China's President Jiang Zemin.

Several hundred supporters were blocked at the borders, and there were 'preventitive' arrests of Iranian dissidents in Paris, prior to Khatami's arrival. Officials claimed that human rights abuses, including the arrest of Iranian Jews as Israeli spies and the detention of student protestors without charge, were on the agenda for discussion, but Iranian officials warned against 'meddling' in domestic affairs. (*International Herald Tribune*)

On 3 November an Amnesty International video, alleging human rights violations in the US, was deemed 'unsuitable' for French television and cinema since it was likely to 'harm good relations among nations'. The Office for Verification of Publicity, which made the decision, has recently prevented campaigns against the human rights records of China and Morocco for the same reason. (*International Herald Tribune*)

On 12 November demonstrators representing the International Concerned Family and Friends of **Mumia Abu-Jamal** occupied the Paris offices of the *International Herald Tribune*, demanding the paper print a petition calling for the retrial of Abu-Jamal. Abu-Jamal is a former Black Panther now on death row for the killing of a Philadelphia policeman. Despite recording recent legal developments in the case and planning a follow-up story, the paper refused to publish the demands of any special interest group. (*International Herald Tribune*)

GEORGIA

President Eduard Shevardnadze condemned the 17 October attack on the Tbilisi offices of the Jehovah's Witnesses by suppporters of a defrocked Georgian Orthodox priest. (RFE/RL)

GERMANY

It was reported on 5 November that a controversial exhibition detailing crimes committed by the army during WWII, is to be closed for about three months following accusations that it falsifies the truth. Independent historians have claimed some photographs in the exhibition are labelled incorrectly, attributing murders committed by Soviet forces to the German army (Wermacht). The exhibition has provoked demonstrations among those incensed at its implicit rejection of the popularly held belief that the Wehrmacht fought an honourable war while the SS retained sole responsibility for war crimes and the Holocaust. (*Guardian*)

On 17 November a court ruling overturned the 1998 conviction of the former head of CompuServe, **Felix Somm**, on 13 cases of illegally distributing child pornography by not blocking customers access to the sites. His defence argued that the technology was not available to block certain sites. (*Daily Telegraph*, Associated Press)

GHANA

On 11 November **Eben Quarcoo**, former editor of the *Free Press* newspaper, was sentenced to 90 days imprisonment after being convicted of libelling President Jerry Rawlings in 1994. Quarcoo was told to choose between paying a fine of 1.5 million cedis (US$600), or spending a further two years in jail. (RSF)

GRENADA

Publisher of the newspaper *Grenada Today* **George Worme** was arrested on 29 September on libel charges, following publication of a letter from an unidentified reader which accused Prime Minister Keith Michell of having bought votes to win the elections. (Associated Press, Freedom Forum)

Freelance journalist **Stanley Charles** turned himself in to police on 1 October, after the media announced that a warrant had been issued for his arrest. Charles is accused of sedition and 'attempting to undermine the country's stability through inflammatory language' during a radio talk show in which he said the prime minister had plotted to kill a former minister. Charles was released on bail. (Associated Press, Freedom Forum)

HAITI

Amnesty International has supported the recent request by UN's independent expert Adama Dieng, urging the US to return intact approximately 160,000 pages of documents confiscated from paramilitary and military headquarters in 1994 by a US-led multinational force sent to restore the democratically elected President Jean Bertrand Aristide to power. In preparation for their return, the documents were transferred to the US Embassy in Port-au-Prince but the government refused to accept them unless they were intact. US authorities have been accused of tampering with the documents where they refer to US citizens and matters relating to US government activities in the state. It is widely believed the documents in question are likely to contain information crucial to investigating past human rights violations. (AI)

INDIA

On 15 October the Supreme Court expressed unhappiness with Narmada Bachao Andolan leader Medha Patkar and author Arundhati Roy for 'knowingly' making 'comments on pending proceedings' and for disobeying interim injunctions in relation to protests and criticisms against the Narmada dam project. Nonetheless, the court, decided not to initiate threatened contempt proceedings against the pair. (*Index* 5/1999). (*Frontline*)

Unknown assailants threw a grenade at the home of the editor of *Afaaq*, **Jeelani Qadri**, on 23 November. No motive for the attack has yet to emerge. (WAN)

INDONESIA

On 27 October an investigation into the embezzlement of billions of dollars of government money by former president Suharto (*Index* 6/1999) was restarted by President Wahid. An investigation was also launched into a bank scandal involving former president Habibie, who was himself responsible for halting the Suharto enquiry. However, on 12 November Wahid promised to pardon Suharto if he were convicted. Such leniency is not expected to extend to Suharto's associates. (*International Herald Tribune*)

IRAN

On 21 October authorities closed the student magazine *Anjoman*, after it carried photos of a violent police attack on student dormitories in Tehran. (Reuters)

Following the banning of *Neshat* on 5 September, its erstwhile editor-in-chief, **Mashallah Shamsolvaezin,** was arrested, tried and jailed on 2 November for having forged the signature for an article opposing the death penalty, despite the author, **Hossein Bagherzade**, freely admitting to having written it. Shamsolvaezin was previously editor of *Jame-eh* and *Tous*, both of which were closed down by the authorities. (HRW)

On 3 November three students, **Mohammad-Reza Namnabati, Abbas Nemati**, and **Ali-Reza Aqaii** were

convicted of publishing a blasphemous play, '*The Entrance Exam and the Time of Resurrection*' (*Index* 6/1999). Each received a suspended sentence. The academic, **Mehdi Sajadehchi**, who permitted the play to be performed in his class was acquitted. A fourth student is awaiting a second hearing. (WiPC, *International Herald Tribune*)

Leading reformist cleric, former interior minister and ally of President Khatami **Abdullah Nouri**, was imprisoned for five years on 28 November for dissent. Nouri was indicted for allegedly using his *Khordad* daily newspaper to insult the Prophet Mohammad, the imams and Ayatollah Khamenei. The high-profile trial was viewed in some quarters as a politically motivated plot to weaken the reformist movement. *Khordad* has since been closed, while Nouri was ordered to pay a fine of 15 million rials (US$8,600) and banned from journalistic activities for a further five years after the completion of his sentence. (*NYT, RSF, International Herald Tribune*)

IRAQ

On 10 November the ministry of information announced that newspapers would soon return to broadsheet format but would remain eight pages long. Economic sanctions had reduced them to tabloid size, and from 16 pages to eight. (*Baghdad Observer*)

JAPAN

In mid-October, the junior defence minister, Shingo Nishimura, was forced to resign following his comments in an interview with *Weekly Playboy* magazine in which he declared the state should consider arming itself with nuclear weapons. Nishimura's inflammatory remarks included the argument that, 'If men were not punished for rape, then we would all be rapists. That is why we need a [nuclear] deterrent.' It is the first time that such a senior member of the government has expressed support for the development of nuclear weapons. (*Guardian*)

Parliament passed a series of bills in November designed to curb the activities of the Aum Shinri Kyo (Supreme Truth) sect, which is accused of the 1995 nerve gas attack on the Tokyo subway system. Although the sect was not directly named in the measures, they target the activities of any group that has engaged in 'indiscriminate mass murder' in the last 10 years. The bills were submitted in response to public demands for government action, amid fears the doomsday cult was staging a comeback. (Reuters)

JORDAN

On 19 October the Press Association (JPA) agreed to abide by its disciplinary committee's decision to expel three journalists involved in 'normalisation' activities with Israel. *Al-Rai*'s columnist **Sultan Hattab**, *Jordan Times*

JORDAN TIMES
'Normalising' free speech

The arrest of two university students trying to launch a website to 'combat normalisation' has important ramifications for our society. Namely, the situation calls upon all concerned authorities to uphold the Constitution and safeguard the rights of those both for and against normalisation.

It is somewhat worrying that the authorities were not more forthcoming in describing the nature of the students' offences in creating the website. Certain parties' tactics in dealing with 'normalisers' – by public degradation and deprivation of their constitutional right to work – is abhorrent. However, their own constitutional right to free speech and opinion must never be denied.

If those students were slandering Jordanians on the website, they should be tried before a court. But, if they were simply expressing a political position, opposed to normalisation for ideological reasons, their arrests are unjustified.

It is striking that the activities and opinions of two university students promulgated on the Internet should draw so much attention while the vast majority of those who threaten and slander Jordanians in the widely-read local press are allowed to continue, unhindered, their activities, many of which surely are of dubious legality.

We, therefore, hope that this is not Jordan's first attempt to censor the Internet, an area in which we have distinguished ourselves from many other countries in terms of access. Due to our dismal record in defending press freedoms, trying to censor the web would only bring us more shame, not to mention such an effort's futility. And considering that there are dozens of Jordanians dedicating spare time and effort to get an ambitious information technology industry off the ground, with the support of the international community, any attempt at censorship sends the wrong message to investors in that sector.

Instead, we appeal to the authorities to focus their efforts on the issue of normalisation, which threatens to be one of the most divisive issues in our society this decade. All Jordanians must try to strike the balance in the preservation of the rights of all. ❏

Jordan's press and government are at loggerheads over the policy of 'normalising' relations with Israel. The only journalists' union has blacklisted members for cross-border contacts which the government positively encourages. In late October, however, two students opposed to normalisation were arrested for launching a website. This was the comment of the English-language Jordan Times *on 28-29 October* chief editor **Abdullah Hasanat** and *al-Dustour* columnist **Jihad Momani** were penalised after their visit to Haifa University's Centre for Arab Jewish Studies. Expulsion from the JPA effectively terminates their journalistic careers. However, on 2 November the expulsion decision was suspended pending consideration of whether the journalists' visit indeed constituted normalisation. (Middle East International, *A19, Jordan Times, Cairo Times*)

In continuing efforts to normalise relations with Israel, the government arrested two university students in the last week of October, for publishing the names of individuals and companies involved in business dealings with the state. (Middle East International)

On 25 November the government proposed a free media zone in the Arab world, in which media institutions would be free from all state laws, provided they did not offend religious values or publish pornography. (*Cairo Times*)

Rebroadcasting of the Russian channel NTV was suspended on 16 October, following a report in the *New York Times* that Swiss authorities investigating money laundering had uncovered an account in the name of President Nursultan Nazarbaev. Who authorised the suspension is unclear, but it appears to have

been ordered by Kazakh Telecom officials keen to please the government. In Almaty, the local rebroadcasting centre chose to black out all Russian channels airing news bulletins. (Internews)

Nursat, the largest Internet provider, formally denied blocking access to the political opposition's Eurasia website. It also affirmed that it neither condoned nor supported any form of Internet censorship. In early November, an unnamed Nursat technician said that access to the Eurasia site would be impossible for an indefinite period due to 'technical reasons'. (RFE/RL, Internews)

Dozens of Uighur women staged a demonstration on 16 November outside the Chinese embassy in Almaty in protest at the continued detention in Xinjiang of **Rebiya Kadeer**. Kadeer was arrested on 11 August (*Index* 6/1999) and charged with involvement with Uighur separatists. (RFE/RL)

Bigeldy Gabdullin, publisher of the independent newspaper *XXI Vek* (21st Century), reported on 18 November that the National Security Committee had ordered the Agricultural Ministry printing house to cease printing the newspaper. Dozens of intellectuals and opposition politicians appealed to President Nazarbaev to intervene on behalf of *XXI Vek*, condemning the refusal by all Almaty publishing houses to print the newspaper as a violation of the constitutionally guaranteed right to freedom of speech. *XXI Vek* was being

printed by the Agricultural Ministry following the unexplained decision, several months earlier, by a commercial printing house to stop printing the newspaper. Condemnation of the crackdown on *XXI Vek* and the independent newspaper *Nachnem s Ponedelnika*, which has faced similar difficulties, was voiced at a meeting of opposition representatives on 1 December. (RFE/RL)

On 3 November *Post on Sunday* publisher, **Tony Gachoka** (*Index* 5/1998, 3/1999), was unexpectedly released from a six-month prison sentence after serving 74 days. Gachoka was imprisoned on 20 August for publishing stories linking President arap Moi to the Goldenberg currency scandal. (Media Institute, Nairobi).

On 29 November the government banned New Zealand journalist **Michael Field** from entering the country, following the publication of articles in which he highlighted the problem of accumulating sewage in Betio. President Teburoro Tito described the articles as 'untruths' and said that Field had been banned for placing the country in a bad light. (Pacific Media Watch)

On 17 October, production of the daily *Al-Siyassa* was suspended for five days

Simon Davies on

PRIVACY

Ursula Owen on

HATE SPEECH

Patricia Williams on

RACE

Gabriel Garcia Marquez on

JOURNALISM

Edward Lucie-Smith on

THE INTERNET

...all in INDEX

SUBSCRIBE & SAVE

UK and overseas

○ **Yes! I want to subscribe to *Index*.**

❏ 1 year (6 issues)   £39   Save 28%
❏ 2 years (12 issues)   £74   Save 31%
❏ 3 years (18 issues)   £102   **You save 37%**

Name

Address

B0B1

£ _____ enclosed.   ❏ Cheque (£)   ❏ Visa/MC   ❏ Am Ex   ❏ Bill me
(*Outside of the UK, add £6 a year for foreign postage*)

Card No.

Expiry   Signature

❏ I do not wish to receive mail from other companies.

INDEX

✉ Freepost: INDEX, 33 Islington High Street, London N1 9BR
☎ (44) 171 278 2313   Fax: (44) 171 278 1878
e tony@indexoncensorship.org

SUBSCRIBE & SAVE

North America

○ **Yes! I want to subscribe to *Index*.**

❏ 1 year (6 issues) $52   Save 21%
❏ 2 years (12 issues) $96   Save 27%
❏ 3 years (18 issues) $135   **You save 32%**

Name

Address

B9B7

$ _____ enclosed.   ❏ Cheque ($)   ❏ Visa/MC   ❏ Am Ex   ❏ Bill me

Card No.

Expiry   Signature

❏ I do not wish to receive mail from other companies.

✉ INDEX, 708 Third Avenue, 8th Floor, New York, NY 10017
☎ (44) 171 278 2313   Fax: (44) 171 278 1878
e tony@indexoncensorship.org

following an article criticising the potential enfranchisement of women. The remarks were deemed an indirect slur on the policies of Sheikh Jaber al-Ahmed al-Sabah. On 31 November Kuwait's all-male parliament threw out a draft law to grant women full political rights from 2003. (CPJ, *Guardian*)

Dr Ahmad al-Baghdadi (*Index* 6/1999) was released on 18 October after serving less than half his one-month jail term. He had been imprisoned for allegedly defaming Islam and the Prophet in a 1996 article. (CPJ)

LEBANON

The trial of songwriter **Marcel Khalife** was postponed until 1 January, to allow his defence more time to prepare. He is charged with having put a verse from the Quran to music (*Index* 6/1999), and faces up to three years' imprisonment if found guilty. (*International Herald Tribune*, HRW)

MALAYSIA

The trial of the imprisoned **Anwar Ibrahim** (*Index* 6/1998, 2/1999, 4/1999, 6/1999) was suspended indefinitely on 15 November. Despite the suspicion that Prime Minister Mahatir Mohammed did 'not want him to be seen in public during the election period', Anwar declared his candidature three days later. (Digital Freedom Network)

Electoral roll irregularities were cited by lawyer Karpal Singh on 16 November as he attempted to sue the government for failing to register 650,000 new voters. The government argues that enrolment was impossible due to the hastily called election. (Reuters)

On 22 November the Chinese language *Sin Chew Jit Poh* apologised for altering a photo from a goverment rally five years earlier, in which the imprisoned former deputy prime minister, **Anwar Ibrahim,** was replaced with the current minister, Abdullah Ahmad Badawi, who held no senior government position at the time. Avoiding the newspaper's 250,000 strong readership, the apology was posted on the Internet, specifically to the forum that discovered the alteration. (*Asiaweek*, *International Herald Tribune*)

On 23 November Alternative Front member Rustam Sani accused government-controlled media of bias in the run-up to the November general election, as opposition parties were verbally told that none of the newspapers would carry their advertisements. The 'unofficial' newspaper *Harakah* (*Index* 3/1992), with a circulation of 320,000, was the only paper to openly print opposition views. It is banned from news-stands and is officially only available to Parti Islam se-Malaysia members. (CPJ)

MEXICO

Amnesty International has called for a full investigation into the circumstances surrounding the discovery of bodies in common graves in Ciudad Juárez. Authorities confirm that on-site forensic work concerned the 'disappearance' of some 100 persons who fell victim to organised drug-traffickers. However, it is believed that some of those 'disappeared' were last seen in the custody of security forces. (AI)

MOZAMBIQUE

Manual Pereira, leader of the main opposition party Renamo, threatened to ban journalists from covering his party in the current general election, after he accused two of them of taking bribes from the Frelimo party. He also criticised state TV (TAM) and the newspaper *Diarion de Mocambique* for biased reporting. (MISA)

NIGERIA

On 11 October Rivers State police arrested **Jerry Needham**, acting editor of the bimonthly *Ogoni Star*, following the leak of a government document detailing police plans to clampdown on ethnic Ijaw activists in the oil-producing Niger Delta. Charged on his day of release, Needham was subsequently granted bail. (CPJ)

Samuel Boyi, a photo-journalist for the state-owned newspaper *Adamawa*, was killed by unidentified bandits when they attacked the convoy of Adamawa state governor Haruna Bonnie. (RSF)

Retired commissioner of police Abubakar Tsav admitted that the investigation into the murder of journalist **Dele Giwa** in 1986, in which two security officers were chief suspects, was quashed from above. The case is currently before the Justice (Chukwudifu) Oputa panel. (*Nigeria Today*)

On 1 December President Obasanjo ordered the arrest of members of the Oodua People's Congress (OPC). Security forces were told to shoot on sight those who resisted such action. This followed civil disturbances in the Lagos suburb of Ketu, in which 90 persons were officially confirmed killed. OPC President **Dr Frederick Fasehun** called the action an attack on Yoruba culture. (*Nigerian Guardian*)

PAKISTAN

On 20 October, the supreme court issued contempt notices to the managing editor of the state-owned television corporation and columnist **Ardesher Cowasjee**. In a programme televised live on 19 October, Cowasjee suggested that accountability in the country should start with the judiciary because it was entirely corrupt. (Pakistan Press Foundation).

On 24 October **Ghulam Farooq**, bureau chief of the English-language daily *Frontier Post*, **Ghafoor Khan** of the local daily *Shamal* and **Muhammad Saleem** of an Urdu-language daily, were arrested and detained for nine

hours following their criticisms of Article 40 in the Frontier Crime Regulations. This 'black law' gave police unlimited powers after the enforcement of *shariah* laws earlier this year, allowing them to harass journalists. The deputy inspector general of police, Sultan Hanif Orakzai, also issued notices against the local and national journalists **Farooq**, **Juma Rehman Afgar**, **Niaz Pashan Jadoon**, **Ali Hazrat Bacha**, **Hamidullah**, **Rehmat Shah Afridi** (*Index* 3/1999, 6/1999), **Syed Ayaz Badshah** and **Hamid Mir** under the same Article. (RSF)

On 19 November a number of journalists and civilians were beaten by police and prevented from entering the anti-terrorism court in Karachi, in which the deposed prime minister, Nawaz Sharif, (*Index* 6/1999) was due to appear. The previous day, the court had directed security staff to allow a limited number of journalists into the court to observe the proceedings. (Pakistan Press Foundation)

In late November **Zahoor Ansari** and **Ayub Khoso**, respectively the chief editor-publisher and columnist for the Sindhi-language daily *Alakh*, were jailed for 17 years. Both men were convicted of publishing derogatory remarks towards the prophets and 'insulting the religious feelings of Muslims', when they used the word 'lust' in a description of the prophets Hazat Nooh, Hazrat Dawood and Hazrat Younas. (RSF)

Recent Publication: *Prison Bound: The denial of Juvenile Justice in Pakistan* (HRW, November 1999, pp 147); *The Kashmir Dispute: Efforts For Its Resolution* by Fahmida Ashraf (Strategic Issues, No. 1, June 1999).

PALESTINE

On 28 November many signatories of a leaflet accusing President Yasser Arafat's administration of 'tyranny, corruption and political deceit', were arrested. Included among those arrested were **Professor Abdul Sattar Qasem**, **Dr Abedel Rahim Kittaneh**, **Dr Adel Samara**, **Dr Yaser Abusafiyya** and **Ahmad Qatameh**, while the former mayors of Nablus and Anabta, **Bassam Shaka'a** and **Waheed Alhamdalla**, were also placed under house arrest. (*Guardian*, Reuters, Associated Press)

PANAMA

A mysterious organisation called the Committee for Freedom of Expression placed posters throughout Panama City depicting *La Prensa* journalist **Gustavo Gorriti** alongside the slogan 'Get to know the assassin of press freedom'. Gorriti's investigative journalism is disliked by many, and in a series of articles, published in August, he revealed suspicious links between the Attorney General José Antonio Sosa, and two US drug traffickers. (CPJ).

PERU

On 8 September the chief of

the Cusco National Food Assistance Programme (PRONAA), Gamaliel Velarde, accused journalist **Fernando Acuña Ortíz** of being a terrorist. Minutes later, a group of PRONAA employees tried to attack the journalist. Acuña had earlier suggested that peasants had been asked to support a re-election campaign in exchange for food. The incident occurred in the local airport after Acuña publicly reprimanded Velarde for forcing mothers that benefited from the 'cup of milk' programme to come to the reception of a minister. (IPYS)

On 20 September **Reynaldo Benavides Ramos**, director and host of the Radio Lurén programme *La Hora Clave*, was stopped by armed individuals and threatened with death if he continued to mess with José Luís Huasasquiche. The journalist had accused Huasasquiche's company of involvement in the failed attempt to assassinate a colleague of his. (IPYS)

The distribution of the 28 September edition of *La República* was prevented and one of its journalists, **Juan Sausa Seclen**, threatened with death. *La República* recently reported on the abuse and intimidation of journalists by Hugo Coral Goycochea, head of the Sixth Military Region intelligence operations unit. (IPYS)

On 14 October the prosecutor of taxation and custom offences recommended four years' imprisonment for **Baruch Ivcher** for fraud and

the misuse of capital resources at Channel 2 television (*Index* 4/1997, 6/1997, 1/1998, 2/1998, 3/1998, 4/1998, 5/1998, 6/1998, 2/1999, 4/1999, 5/1999). The manager of the station, **Alberto Cabello Ortega** and two Venezuelan businessmen, Jesus Trapiello Gonzalez and Cesar Diaz Belisario, were also sentenced to four and three years in prison respectively for their role in the incident. (IPYS)

The journalist **Angel Durán León**, accused of contempt, was given a one-year suspended prison sentence and fined 5,000 nuevos soles (US$1,450) in civil damages, payable to Vice-Minister Fredy Moreno. León, of Radio Quassar, has faced over 15 legal charges from Moreno and been cleared on fourteen occasions. (IPYS)

On 20 October the director of the daily *El Tío*, **José Olaya**, was threatened with death. In November 1996 Olaya was attacked by two unidentified, armed individuals. (IPYS)

On 27 October, the former editor of the daily *El Chato*, **Hugo Borjas**, was kidnapped and threatened with a knife by unknown individuals. Borjas had previously stated that the government was paying the newspaper to publish defamatory statements against the main opposition presidential candidates. One week earlier, ex-employees of the sensationalist daily revealed that the owner, Rafael Documet, had been paid US$180,000 a month to

publish headlines and offensive articles against opposition politicians and journalists. (IPYS)

On 10 November the Radio Quassar reporter **Cesar Romero** was shot in a leg when he and the driver of the vehicle in which he was travelling were forced to remove some stones left in middle of the road. (IPYS)

On 22 November the daily *Referendum* began publishing again with a completely new staff and a new openly pro-government line. The owners claimed to have sacked all independent journalists due to financial problems. (IPYS)

PHILIPPINES

The *Manila Times* resumed a pro-Estrada tack after 30% of its stock was bought by Marcel Crespo and another 40% divided among the President's associates. The paper began publishing again on 25 October, but its housing and computer chiefs left soon after, following the publication of apparent criticism of Estrada. (*Asiaweek*)

President Joseph Estrada's insidious grip on the media increased in November, with three new weekly radio programmes, commencing on each of the most popular national stations, complementing the weekly radio-TV show where he explains policy initiatives and reactions to events. (*Asiaweek*)

The advertising boycott against the *Philippine Daily*

Inquirer (*Index* 5/1999), was lifted on 22 November, three days after the newspaper's president **Alexandra Pietro** and editor **Letty Jimenez-Magsanoc** had dinner with Estrada's son. Editorial staff are to receive manuals on 'fair, accurate and balanced reporting'. (*Asia Week*)

ROMANIA

On 28 September the European Court of Human Rights ruled that the government violated Articles 10, (freedom of expression) and six (fair trial) of the European Convention of Human Rights in its management of the case of **Ionel Dalban**. Following the 1992 publication of an article about a series of frauds, allegedly committed by the chief executive of state-owned agricultural company Dalban, the manager of the magazine *Cronica Romascana* was found guilty of 'criminal libel' and sentenced to three months' imprisonment. The European Court ruled that his conviction was unnecessary 'in a democratic society' as his articles concerned matters of public interest in the management of state assets. Dalban died in March 1998 and his widow was awarded 250,000,000 lei (US$14,000) by the European Court. (IPI)

RUSSIAN FEDERATION

On 20 November the Legislative Assembly of the Republic of Bashkortostan cancelled broadcasts of a controversial analytical programme, hosted by Sergei

Dorenko and the Zerkalo programme, from Russian Public Television (ORT). The decree was issued on the grounds that both shows violated 'federal and republic' election laws. In the past Dorenko has hosted a number of programmes focusing on Moscow Mayor Yuri Luzhkov's financial dealings. (RFE/RL)

On 31 October NTV broadcast that **Atis Klimovics**, a correspondant with *Diena*, was in Chechnya and in danger of being kidnapped by rebel forces. However, later that day, he appeared on the Latvian television news programme 'Panorama' and informed viewers that he had left Chechnya one week earlier. He said there were severe obstacles preventing journalists from covering events in the region and that the authorities were happy with 'journalists' reports that diverge from the views of the information center created especially for this war in Moscow.' (RFE/RL)

On 18 November the offices of independent Radio Lemma were shut down by Yevgeni Nazdratenko, governor of Primorsky Krai in eastern Russia. The official reason for the closure was violation of a rental agreement, but journalists say that airtime given to the governor's political opponent **Viktor Cherepkov** was more likely to have been the real motivation. On 19 November Cherepkov, the former Vladivostok mayor, pulled out of the elections because Nazdratenko's actions

were preventing clean elections. Nazdratenko arranged for the dismissal of the editor of *Moskovskii Komsomolets* in Vladivostok, who he considered to have been too critical of his administration. It was also reported on 20 November that authorities prevented the opposition newspaper, *Arsenieveskie Vesti*, from publishing. (RFE/RL)

On 23 November the state Duma refused to reconsider an earlier resolution, passed on 19 November, ordering the seizure of ORT's bank account. The state has a controlling 51% share in ORT but Boris Berezovsky, who is expected to run for the Duma, is the most influential private shareholder. Valdimir Ryzhkov, leader of Our Home is Russia (NDR), said that the 19 November decision grossly violated Duma regulations as some members voted on behalf of absent colleagues, since many members of NDR and Liberal Democratic Party had been absent on that day. The resolution followed complaints by the Audit Chamber that ORT was not allowing it to conduct financial investigations The station was also accused of faking footage of Moscow police in order to discredit the city's mayor, Yuri Luzhkov. (RFE/RL)

On 17 November **Andrei Yrgonyants**, a correspondent in Belgorode province for the Moscow newspaper *Komsomolskaya Pravda*, was beaten by military officers while returning from a meeting with the provincial administration. He was detained at the Fourth Militia department of Belgorod, but eventually taken to the city hospital where he was found to be suffering from stomach trauma and injuries to his thorax and kidneys. (GDF)

In the 'closed town' of Snezhinsk, **Nikolai Schoor**, editor-in-chief and writer for the human rights newspaper *Ecology*, stood trial on 30 November. He is accused of libel in two articles, the first regarding local state environmental institutions and the second which questions the existence and legality of the 'closed towns', which were established as centres of nuclear, military and scientific research. Following the withdrawal of Schoor's lawyer, due to a conflict of interests after her recent marriage to a senior local bureaucrat, the judged decided to postpone the trial until 27 December. (Ecology)

RWANDA

During late November authorities denied an entrance visa to **Carla de Ponte**, prosecutor of the international war crimes tribunal investigating the massacre of Tutsis in 1994. The Tutsi-dominated government was reportedly angered at the decision to drop charges of genocide against Jean-Bosco Barayagawiza on a technicality. (*International Herald Tribune*)

SERBIA-MONTENEGRO

Dan Graf, the company which publishes the Belgrade-based

independent daily *Danes*, has been fined 280,000 dinars ($US29,00), and its director, **Dusan Mitrovic**, fined 80,000 dinars ($US7,100) by the capital's Municipal Court for four breaches of Article 69 of the Public Information Act. The ruling on 26 October followed a complaint by Deputy Prime Minister Voljislav Seselj that the newspaper had published an article which wrongly attributed to him a statement given by Deputy Montenegrin Prime Minister Norvak Kilibarda. The heavy fines may lead to the closure on the firm. (RSF, ANEM)

On 28 October a Belgrade court fined **Cedomir Jovanovic** 320,000 dinars ($US28,500) for distributing *Promene* (Change), a bulletin of the opposition movement Alliance for Change. The editor was found guilty of circulating an unregistered periodical after *Promene* was deemed to be a public newspaper. Alliance of Change representatives protested that the bulletin was publicity material distributed at its protest rallies and did not need to be registered. However, the ministry failed to explain the justification of its classification. Javanovic's fine was paid by a new organisation unconnected to the Alliance for Change, calling itself Team 29. (ANEM, RFE/RL)

On 1 November **Dessa Trevisan**, a British journalist for *The Times*, was sentenced to 10 days' imprisonment for illegally entering the country. Despite having a valid and

current visa, she was found guilty of travelling without an entry stamp in her passport. Her lawyer, who will appeal against the decision, blamed the police for not stamping her passport at the border with Montenegro. (RFE/RL, RSF)

Radio Free Montenegro was allowed to resume bradcasting on 15 November after the station was banned by the Montenegrin government for lacking 'technical documentation'. According to editor-in-chief **Nebojsa Redzic**, the closure was motivated by the station's ties with the opposition Liberal Party and its broadcast of reports critical of certain ministers in Milo Djukanovic's government. During the NATO air strikes, Redzic had to seek exile abroad as Radio Free Montenegro faced reprisals for broadcasting international radio programmes. (RSF, RFE/RL)

The Belgrade weekly *Nedeljni Telegraf* was fined 160,000 dinars ($US14,200) on 24 November for publishing an article entitled 'Why is the Yugoslav River Shipping Company, a firm of national importance, falling into ruins.' The charges were brought by the director of the shipping company Dusan Stupar. (B2-92)

A rock concert in Bor by the group Sunshine was broken up on 27 November. Police vacated the club where the concert was held, searching fans and the premises in the process. The concert was part of a tour organised by the

• •

THE JOURNALISTS OF NEZAVISNE NOVINE

Whose language?

We, the journalists and editors of *Nezavisne Novine*, live and work under extraordinary circumstances. We use a language which is unique in its wealth of nuance. Every language is wonderful in its own way and sufficient for those who only wish to use it to tell the truth.

But language is only the means. The basic question is who is using it, to what ends and with what skill? Our inheritance is such that this magnificent language is used mostly for propaganda, rather than to inform people about what is actually happening.

We have tried to inform people but it is not easy to face the truth. On the contrary, for the people of this country, this has been a painful and traumatic experience. However, it is a necessary experience; a kind of sobering up, without which there would be no future.

For those who use our beautiful language for demagoguery, to convince everyone that everything is OK when, in fact, they themselves are the only ones who are OK, our road back to consciousness represents a direct attack on their interests. Now the whole world knows how they have reacted.

This prize, as well as the thousands of telegrams, messages and letters of support from those who unmistakably agree with us, has confirmed that we are, without doubt, on the right road. We chose our road a long time ago: it is a bitter path, but one we have to take to achieve catharsis. ❏

On 22 October Zeljko Kopanja, owner and editor of the Banja Luka newspaper Nezavisne Novine, *lost both legs in a car bomb attack. The attempted assassination appeared to be linked to articles the paper published detailing the mass killing of 200 Bosnian Muslims in August 1992 at the Koricani cliffs on Mount Vlasic. In a statement issued after the bomb,* Nezavisne Novine *and* Radio Nes, *which Kopanja also owns, said they would maintain the same editorial approach. On 30 November the staff of* Nezavisne Novine *were awarded the* Index on Censorship *Freedom of the Press award. This is an edited version of their acceptance speech*

• •

Association of Independent Electronic Media (ANEM) and began the 'Silence Won't Do' campaign. In addition to the concerts, experts in media freedom and human rights are to discuss the consequences of continuous repression. (ANEM, B2-92)

SOUTH AFRICA

On 19 October Reuters suspended its television operation in Cape Town following threatening phone calls to the agency. No detail of threats was given by the senior managers in London, who took the decision. (MISA)

The 'Interim Report of the Inquiry into Racism in the Media', published by the South African Human Rights Commission (SAHRC) on 22 November, severely criticised the press for partiality and racism. Editors and journalists have been ordered to respond to the report within 30 days or the commission will subpoena them to give evidence at public hearings scheduled for next year. (South African Human Rights Commission)

SOUTH KOREA

The Media Rating Board rejected Stanley Kubrick's movie *Eyes Wide Shut* by declining to give it a viewing rating. Scenes in which actors perform group sex were deemed too offensive for viewing. Kubrick's 1987 film *Full Metal Jacket* was also initially rejected by the board for nudity. It was eventually shown uncut several years later. (Reuters)

SRI LANKA

On 6 November, after a week of military defeats at the hands of the Tamil Tigers, the government's information department prohibited 'the publication, broadcast or transmission of sensitive military information'. The ban is intended to close all possible loopholes in existing censorship legislation (*Index* 4/1998). (Associated Press, CPJ)

On the same day **Ramesh Nadarajah**, the Eelam People's Democratic Party (EPDP) MP and chief editor of the Tamil-language weekly *Thinamurasu,* was shot dead by an unknown assailant. Analysts in Colombo cite Nadarajah's recent switch to hard-line Tamil nationalism and support for the Liberation Tigers of Tamil Eelam as possible motives for his murder. (Associated Press, RSF)

SUDAN

On 31 October opposition politician **Dr Kadouda** found his teenage daughter beaten unconscious on the floor of his home. A note next to her body said the attack was intended as a warning. In the months preceding, Dr Kadouda had received a number of threats of violence and warnings of retaliation should he denounce the government and publicly advocate his support for democracy in the country. Police have, so far, failed to investigate the case. (HRW)

SWAZILAND

The furore surrounding the arrest and forced resignation of former *Times Sunday* editor **Bheki Makhubu** (*Index* 6/1999) has led the government to review its proposed anti-defamation bill. (A19)

The condition of imprisoned human rights activist Nizar Nayouf has further deteriorated (*Index* 6/1999). (HRW)

SYRIA

On 23 November **Nizar Nayouf** was awarded the World Association of Newspapers 2000 Golden Pen of Freedom prize. Nayouf, the editor-in-chief of *Voice of Democracy* and Secretary-General of the Committee for the Defence of Democratic Freedom, has been imprisoned since 1992 and is said to be 'near death due to torture and the effects of diseases for which he has been denied adequate treatment'. (WAN)

TAJIKISTAN

Government media restrictions left only one independent newspaper remaining to cover the run-up to the 6 November presidential election. An outright ban on opposition media, imposed during the 1992-97 civil war during which around 80 journalists were killed, was only lifted by the government in August 1999. Members of the United Opposition (UTO) did not appear on state-controlled radio or television during the election campaign and efforts by UTO members to express themselves in the print media were severely curtailed. Opposition politicians outside the UTO appeared to have been denied any access to the media. Harassment from the authorities forced the only Dushanbe newspaper to have printed the views of the UTO to close in mid-October 1999, leaving just one other remaining to print substantial political information. Opposition candidate **Davlat Usmon** attempted to withdraw from the election in protest, but officials ensured that his name remained on the ballot paper, to bolster their claims of a free election. At his swearing-in ceremony on 16 November, President Imomali Rakhmonov, who won 96% of the vote, placed political pluralism and media freedom among 'the most important objectives' of his second term. The US, EU and OSCE all condemned the conduct of the election and expressed concern for the February 2000 parliamentary vote. (HRW, RFE/RL)

TANZANIA

On 20 October the Christian Revival (TCR) organisation announced it would sue the weekly religious newspaper *Msemakweli* for defamation. The TCR is seeking Tsh300m shillings (US$37,500) in damages, as a result of several articles inciting 'hatred, ridicule and damaging the reputation of the TCR'. Francis Msangi of the TCR claimed that for several weeks the weekly tabloid had been

'insisting the TCR was a Christian organisation that broke up marriages'. (MISA)

Ambokele Malele was arrested in Arusha on 4 November and 16 of his tapes, which he was selling at the time, were confiscated. Reverend **Christopher Mtikila**, who heads the unregistered Democratic party and is known for recording speeches and diatribes against opposition politicians, was also arrested on 9 November. Both were charged with publishing words with seditious intent and inciting dissastisfaction with the government. Their cases were adjourned to 29 November. In the last year at least 19 newspapers have been cautioned by the government due to their content. Minister of State for Information Muhammed Seif Khatib is currently threatening papers with deregistration if they publish obscene articles or cartoons with a negative social impact. (MISA)

TUNISIA

On 21 October authorities banned the distribution of the French daily *Le Monde.* Between January and June 1999, 14 issues of the daily were barred from distribution in the state. In another related development authorities also suspended the broadcast of television station France2 on 25 October, following its critical coverage of the political issues. (RSF)

TURKEY

On 21 September the writer

and sociologist **Ismail Besikci** (*Index* 5/1999) who was serving sentences amounting to 79 years in jail, was released as part of a recent amnesty (*Index* 6/1999). Besikci, 62, has spent a total of 18 years in prison for his writings on Kurdish issues. The amnesty law, however, only suspended the sentence for 3 years, allowing a return to prison should he publish controversial material in that time. (Reuters, BBC News, WAN)

Akin Birdal (*Index* 4/1998, 5/1998, 1/1999, 4/1999, 6/1999) the former president of the Human Rights Association was temporarily freed from prison on 23 September after the EU urged a release on medical grounds. Birdal survived an assassination attempt last May, when he was shot six times in the chest and leg, but is still suffering from severe injuries. (Washington Kurdish Institute, Reuters)

On 20 October issue 53 of the monthly Kurdish journal *Deng* (Voice) was confiscated in Istanbul. The monthly was withheld for articles deemed to 'violate the indivisibility of the state' by claiming the existence of a Kurdish people. (*Deng* Press Statement, *Info-Turk*)

Prominent academic and journalist **Ahmet Taner Kislali** was assassinated outside his home in Ankara on 21 October. The former culture minister died from wounds sustained when he tried to remove a disguised bomb from his windscreen. Police suspect Islamic extremist groups, although no organisation has yet claimed responsibility for the attack. (IFJ, CPJ, IPI)

On 30 September two members of the Izmir branch of the Human Rights Foundation were detained and beaten by gendarmes. Psychiatrist **Dr Alp Ayan** and secretary **Gunseli Kaya** were arrested after participating in a demonstration at the funeral of **Nevzat Ciftci**, one of 10 prisoners murdered in Ankara Central Prison. Witnesses reported that Dr Ayan was severely beaten and his car destroyed by the military police. Both are to stand trial for terrorist propaganda. (AAASHRAN)

On 1 November a local radio station was ordered off the air for 30 days after broadcasting a BBC news report. Radio Foreks was banned by the state-run radio and television watchdog RTUK for running a live news bulletin from the BBC's Turkish Section. The RTUK said that the ban was enforced because the service was 'essentially giving the terrorist organisation the Kurdistan Workers Party (PKK) a political identity'. (Reuters)

On 11 November the newspaper *Ozgur Bakis* (*Index* 5/1999) was fined and closed for nine days. The pro-Kurdish daily was charged with publishing news stories deemed to be 'against national security'. The newspaper's owner, **Halis Dogan** and **Cihan Sapan**, its editor-in-chief, were convicted for printing the statements of Cemil Bayak, an executive

member of the presidency council of the PKK. (Evrensel, TIHV, *Info-Turk*)

The series of trials against the 'Freedom of Thought Initiative' continued on 10 November at a military court in Istanbul. Charged with writings in the booklet 'Freedom of Thought-38', **Sanar Yurdatapan** (*Index* 1/1997, 3/1998, 5/1998, 6/1998, 2/1999) refused to defend his case on the grounds that military courts should not try civilians. (*Info-Turk*)

Kurdish singer **Mehmet Besir Guzel** was sentenced to 10 months' imprisonment, on 14 November after he sang a Kurdish song at a fund-raising benefit organised by the Diyarbakir branch of the Association of Physically Handicapped Persons to collect money for victims of the recent earthquake. The evidence presented at the trial included the use of the words *kesk* (green), *sor* (red), and *zer* (yellow) and 'Kurdistan' in the song. These are regarded as the Kurdish national colours. The sentence was suspended for five years. (*Ozgur Bakis*)

A court ended the case against the US journalist **Andrew Finkel** (*Index* 5/1999) on 16 November by invoking a government amnesty for people convicted or charged for their writings. Finkel, who insisted on a formal dismissal of the charges on the grounds that the amnesty had deprived him of the chance to clear his name, pointed out that the sentence had merely been suspended for three years. He

was charged with insulting the army in an article he wrote about Sirnak, a town in the Kurdish region of the state of emergency Area. (Associated Press)

Kanal 21 television station was banned by the RTUK from broadcasting for one year on 24 November. Kanal 21 executive board member **Ibrahim Sucu** said that the ban was apparently ordered following the broadcast of a song by popular Kurdish singer, **Sivan Perwar**, which the RTUK claimed contained words of an incendiary nature. (*Kurdish Observer, Ozgur Politika*)

The president of the Turkish Association for Human Rights was attacked and beaten up by extreme right activists on 25 November in Ankara. **Husnu Ondul** and Assistant General Secretary **Avni Kalkan** were attacked by the assailants, including one woman, who had been dropped off outside the office building by four police vans. Police waited on the steps outside but did not intervene. (*Info-Turk*)

An interpreter who translated speeches into Kurdish at a cultural festival was sentenced to 10 months' imprisonment on 1 December. **Fahime Aslan**, an employee of the Adana branch of the Kurdish association Mesopotamia Cultural Centre, had been the translator at a 'Festival for Solidarity with the People' in late 1998. (*Kurdish Observer, Ozgur Politika*)

TURKMENISTAN

Ashgabat City authorities bulldozed the state's only Seventh Day Adventist church on 13 November. President Niyazov had only granted permission for the construction of the church in 1992. Officials also raided an Evangelical Baptist community in Ashgabat on 14 November, confiscating Bibles and hymn books. (RFE/RL, Compass Direct)

UK

An election modernisation bill, announced in the Queen's Speech on 20 October, stated that the mentally ill and prisoners on remand will be given the vote. Under the home secretary's proposals, which are expected to become law next year, mentally ill patients will be allowed to use a hospital as a registered address. Traditionally, 'criminals, lunatics and peers' have been the only groups denied the vote: the new legislation will only bar convicted criminals. Hereditary peers who lost their seats in the recent reform of the House of Lords are also expected to be enfranchised. (Daily Telegraph)

In a radical new attempt to cut crime, it was announced on 24 October that anyone who is arrested and taken to a police station will be tested for alcohol, regardless of whether the offence is drink-related. Those who fail to comply with the order will be refused bail. Suspects found to be over the drink-driving limit will also be urged to undertake an alcohol awareness course. There are also plans to introduce compulsory drugs testing and DNA sampling. (Daily Telegraph)

On 24 October it was reported that the Foreign Office had briefed the Metropolitan police about Chinese government concerns about the impact of demonstrations during the state visit of President Jiang Zemin (Index 6/1999). The admission fuelled claims that the government told police to take a hard line with demonstrators and encouraged a policy of 'zero tolerance'. Foreign Office spokesman John Battle confirmed that meetings took place with the Metropolitan Police, some of which were attended by Chinese Embassy staff. However, there were no minutes to confirm or deny the allegation. (Daily Telegraph)

On 27 October Ed Maloney's decision not to pass his interview notes with William Stobie, concerning the murder of human rights lawyer Pat Finucane, to the investigating team led by John Stevens was upheld by Sir Robert Carsell, Lord Chief Justice of Northern Ireland (Index 6/1999). Maloney, Northern editor of the Sunday Tribune was facing imprisonment for his stand. However the ruling said that the police had failed to show that the notes would be of substantial value to their inquiry. (Guardian, CPJ)

On 1 November Richard Horton editor of The Lancet, one of Britain's leading medical journals, said he had been threatened by a senior member of the Royal Society. The threat was thought to have been in connection with his intention to publish a controversial report that questioned the safety of genetically modified food. The threat came during an aggressive telephone call in which he was told that, if he published the research, it would 'have implications for his personal position' as editor. Following the call, Horton immediately informed his colleagues and was able to name the caller. (Guardian)

In early November a group of Muslims issued a fatwa against the playwright Terrence McNally for depicting Jesus Christ as a homosexual in Corpus Christi. The group said that McNally would face arrest and execution if he travelled to Muslim countries. (International Herald Tribune)

On 8 November it was reported that the Lord Chancellor's department had closed James Hulbert's website because it contained material that criticised judges. Since his acquital for assault and deception, for which he won an out of court settlement, Hulbert has pursued a legal battle to force the courts to accept that some of the material used against him was fabricated. His Internet service provider, Kingston Internet, informed him that his webspace was 'being disabled with immediate effect', after a complaint from the Lord Chancellor's department. The company justified its action by claiming

NICOLAS WALTER
An open letter

Bryan Magee has been an academic and politician and is also an author and broadcaster. His intellectual autobiography, *Confessions of a Philosopher: A Journey Through Western Philosophy* (1997),which has been published on both sides of the Atlantic, includes a chapter, On Knowing Russell, which concludes with a passage about Ralph Schoenman, a close associate of Bertrand Russell during the 1960s.

This passage is certainly very critical of Schoenman, but it adds nothing to what was spoken and written at the time. The stories of his manipulation of Russell and rudeness to Russell's friends, and the theories about his suspected position as an agent of sinister political interests, were widely circulated during the 1960s and are mentioned in Ronald Clark's biography, *The Life of Bertrand Russell* (1975); indeed the most critical account appears in Russell's own *Private Memorandum concerning Ralph Schoenman* (1970).

Nevertheless, following legal action by Ralph Schoenman, it was agreed in the High Court of Justice in London on 10 November 1999 that the author and publishers of the book should make an apology, pay 'substantial damages' (estimated at £100,000) and legal costs, and destroy all unsold copies of the book. Thousands of people had already read the book and millions have now seen reports of the case. However, this unscrupulous use of the civil law of defamatory libel not only penalises the author and publisher, but prevents other people from making up their own minds.

Ralph Schoenman's relationship with Bertrand Russell and his general political conduct remain matters of genuine public interest, and their open discussion neither should nor could be obstructed. A transcript of the relevant section of the book will be sent to anyone who requests it. For copies write, enclosing a stamped addressed envelope, to the Free Speech Movement, 84b Whitechapel High Street, London E1 7QX. ❑

Nicolas Walter *is a journalist and lecturer, who has just retired after 25 years with the Rationalist Press Association* that the site breached its 'terms and conditions'. (*Guardian*)

A Consumers Association poll, published in early November, said that 94% of the public did not trust ministers to release information and that they wanted their 'right to know' enshrined in law. The poll showed that Home Secretary Jack Straw's promise to end the 'culture of secrecy' with his new Freedom of Information Act has failed to impress the public. The bill contains large omissions including blanket bans on releasing information used to formulate policy, and allowing ministers to hide behind commercial secrecy if they choose not to release information. The poll also found that 85% of people questioned believed that the public's right to know should outweigh the commercial interests of companies or public authorities. (*Guardian*)

On 12 November **Andrei Cherkasov** of NTV, **Alexander Panov** of ORT and their unnamed cameraman were beaten up by Islamic radicals at a rally in London to support and raise money for Chechen forces. Vladimir Rakmanin, a Russian foreign ministry spokesman, said the attack was 'an outrageous incident', especially since the police stood by during the assault by the predominantly Muslim crowd. (*Daily Telegraph*, RFE/RL)

On 1 December an anti-drink driving leaflet, featuring a photograph of the car crash which killed Diana, Princess of Wales, was withdrawn by

Ministry of Defence (MoD) police. The leaflet, which bore the warning 'Unfortunately even a princess isn't safe with a drink driver', was handed out to visitors to RAF Alconbury. An MoD spokesman said the advert was distasteful and a silly mistake, which he hoped would not deflect people from following the campaign throughout the country. (Press Association)

UKRAINE

Between 13 and 15 October printing houses in the cities of Kryviy Rih and Luhansk refused to print four newspapers that endorsed President Leonid Kuchma's political rivals. *XXI Vek* could not be published after its editor, **Yuri Yurov**, refused to remove both a front page photo of opposition candidate Yevhen Marchuk and several articles critical of Kuchma's administration. In the same week two other newspapers, *Rankurs* and *Nashe Zavtra*, which both endorsed the candidate Alexandre Moroz were unable to go to print. Rankurs' usual publishing company claimed it was experiencing 'technical problems', while the printer that publishes *Nashe Zavtra* had been shut down by tax inspectors. On 15 October employees at a state-owned printing house told the editors of *Kryvoi Rog Vecherny* that they were breaking their contract. One of the editors, Inna Chyrchenko was detained and questioned for 17 hours about the paper's political ties, after police ransacked the offices. It has also recently

experienced a series of hostile tax investigations. (CPJ)

In the run-up to the presidential elections a number of journalists experienced harassment and intimidation. *Chornomorsky Noviny* journalist **Leonid Zveerev** began receiving death threats towards himself and his family from 4 October onwards. Secret services offered him 'protection' on the condition that he agreed to be less critical of local authorities. The following day *Postup* editor **Orest Drul** said that three strangers tried to break into his apartment after the newspaper published a series of reports criticising the local government in Lviv. Meanwhile TV Simon chairman **Alexandre Davtian** and journalist **Zurab Aslania** both received death threats. Aslania was also told on 10 October that she would be killed a month after the election, while her family were threatened with deportation by the police after her investigation into allegations of corruption involving people close to the President. (CPJ)

On 15 September **Vuriy Nesteerenko**, a journalist with the public television channel UT1, resigned after one of his reports was manipulated and libellous elements added with the intention of compromising an opposition candidate. In a similar incident **Viktor Borissov**, presenter of the television programme *Picentre-debaty* on the private channel Vikka, was forced to resign on 18 October, following a live interview with the opposition candidate Alexandre Moroz. The programme was suspended on the same day it was due to host several presidential candidates, because the presenter was 'unwell'. (RSF, CPJ)

USA

On 18 October journalist **Terry Allen** was released from her freelance duties, following the publication of her revelations that Indonesian students at a private military college in Vermont had links to the Indonesian army's notorious special forces. Her ex-employers, the publishers of local Vermont papers, the *Burlington Free Press* and the *Rutland Herald*, both rejected the story, so she took it to the *Boston Globe*, which put it on the front page. The accuracy of the story is not in doubt, but a college donor, R. John Mitchell, is the publisher of the papers in question. (*Boston Globe*)

By 22 October US mainstream media continued to ignore an investigative article published in the UK *Observer* on 17 October which reported that Nato deliberately bombed the Chinese embassy in Belgrade last May. **John Sweeney**'s story, which claimed that the embassy was bombed because it was relaying Yugoslav military radio signals, appeared in other international news sources and caused German Chancellor Gerhard Schroeder to publicly question Nato's version of the incident. US media have faithfully adhered to Nato's explanation that the

bombing was accidental because it was based on an 'outdated map'. (Fair News)

On 2 November scientists and drug companies involved in gene therapy research admitted that they had failed to inform the National Institute of Health of six research-related deaths over the past 19 months. The deaths, which resulted from attempts to grow new blood vessels around blocked ones, are the first in gene therapy research to have been deliberately withheld from federal bodies. (*International Herald Tribune*)

On 2 November a federal judge rescinded the punishment meted out to the Brooklyn Museum of Art for its 'Sensation' exhibition (*Index* 6/1999). Millions of dollars of funding, halted following the initial decision, were ordered restored by District Judge Nina Gershon, who concluded that the museum had a strong 'likelihood of success on its First Amendment claim'. (*International Herald Tribune*)

On 5 November Kansas teacher **Stan Roth** was sacked after 40 years' service for calling the teaching of creationism 'non-scientific crap'. The decision came a few weeks before the state board of education was due to remove all evolution from the compulsory curriculum. Asked by a 16-year-old, Christian fundamentalist pupil 'when are we going to learn about creationism,' Roth claims he replied, 'when are you going to stop believing that crap your parents teach you?' He has

been defended by former pupils and other teachers. (*Daily Telegraph*)

On 9 November the army attempted to stop a TV advertisement for presidential candidate John McCain in which he is shown walking solemnly through Arlington National Cemetery. An army spokesman said that, even if any request had been made to film the advert, it would have been declined on the grounds that 'partisan activity' of any kind is banned at all army installations. McCain is a former navy pilot who was shot down and taken prisoner during the Vietnam War. (*International Herald Tribune*)

On 12 November Pacifica Radio's national news director **Dan Coughlin** was removed from his post days after airing a brief, factual report on a nationwide boycott of the station. In protest, the only African-American national news anchor in public broadcasting, Verna Avery Brown, has refused to appear on air since. In a direct protest to the station's directors, local Pacifica staff in New York and Berkeley said the incident was deplorable.' (Fair News)

On 16 November the American Civil Liberties Union (ACLU) began a campaign to focus public attention on the threats to civil liberties which are posed by Project Echelon, an intelligence-gathering network led by the National Security Agency and comprising other agencies from the United Kingdom, Canada, Australia and New Zealand (*Index* 5/1998). The most powerful creation of its kind, it has the ability to capture electronic communications worldwide and identify certain subjects through keywords. Echelon became prominent when the European Parliament received two reports detailing its operations. (ACLU)

On 18 November it was reported that the mail order Internet company Amazon.com, had been shipping an extraordinary number of copies of Adolf Hitler's manifesto *Mein Kampf* to customers in Germany. While it is illegal to publish or sell the book in Germany, ordering *Mein Kampf* by mail is perfectly legal and, consequently, resulted in the book reaching Amazon's top 10 best-seller list for Germany during the summer. Following pressure from the Simon Wiesenthal Centre, Amazon ceased shipping the book outside of the US. (*International Herald Tribune*)

On 19 November analysts said the announcement of a news-sharing alliance between the *Washington Post*, *Newsweek* magazine and NBC News will produce inevitable conflicts of interest. NBC is jointly owned by weapons contractor General Electric, in partnership with Microsoft. The *Post*'s executive editor, Leonard Downie Jr, gave the assurance that this would not change or colour our coverage'. (*International Herald Tribune*)

A Washington businessman, Leo Smith, who became so

frustrated by the failure to impeach President Clinton, that he set up a website to urge voters to replace his congressional representative, faces legal action because of the cost of the website. The site was added to his business website on a business computer and so only cost his time but has been valued at more than US$250, at which value the author must disclose his identity. Having been informed by the FEC that he faced possible legal action, he dared them to try, saying 'if you can't advocate what you want for an election, that strikes at the heart of our democracy'. (ACLU)

The *New England Journal of Medicine* was found to have broken its own code of conduct after *Los Angeles Times* research showed that writers for the magazine, which is relied upon by millions of doctors worldwide for impartial advice, had financial links to drug-producing companies. Of a series of 36 articles, authors or co-authors of eight had financial links to at least one of the companies whose product was being assessed, it was reported on 22 October. Financial links to drug manufacturers are banned. (*Daily Telegraph*)

UZBEKISTAN

In mid-November Talib Yakubov, general secretary of the Human Rights Society, told a UN human rights panel that authorities have built a huge prison camp in the southwest desert of the Aral Sea, where they are

incarcerating people for their religious beliefs. According to Yakubov, 38 prisoners have died at the camp so far this year. (RFE/RL)

Forty women protested outside the Tashkent mayor's office on 18 November in protest at the arrest of male relatives on charges of possessing illicit Islamic literature produced by the group *Hizb-ut-Tahrir*. The women claim that the charges against the men, all practising Muslims, have been fabricated. Officials videotaped the protest and took down protesters' names. After the protest was disbanded, plainclothes officers assumed to be from the National Security Service followed several of the women as they entered a nearby Metro station. (HRW, RFE/RL)

On 18 November **Komil Bekjanov**, younger brother of exiled opposition leader **Muhammad Solih**, disappeared while in state custody. Bekjanov, who is serving a 10-year sentence following his conviction in a widely condemned trial for the possession of narcotics and weapons, was last seen on 12 July. Family members have searched for him from prison to prison but have received no information on his whereabouts, except that he was reportedly moved from Urgench prison on 18 July 1999. Bekjanov was initially detained on 19 February (*Index* 3/1999) during the authorities' swoop on associates of dissidents following the February bombings in Tashkent. (HRW)

VATICAN

On 5 November it was announced that the beatification of Pope Pius XII would be delayed. Accused by critics of being shamefully silent during the Holocaust, he is revered as a saint by many in the Roman Catholic Church. In his recent book, *Hitler's Pope: The Secret History of Pius XII,* John Cornewell revived the public scrutiny of the wartime religious leader. The intensity of the dispute has caused many religious scholars to question the decision to nominate him for sainthood. Some Jewish organisations have suggested the delay is a result of their direct lobbying. Nonetheless, the Vatican said the 'beatification of Pius XII will not take place in the year 2000 because we have not completed the preparatory work, but that does not mean it has been slowed or stopped.' (*International Herald Tribune*)

VIETNAM

Speaking from Vermont on 17 October, Zen Buddhist monk **Thich Nhat Hanh** made a plea for reconciliation with Hanoi and requested the freedom to return to his home country. Thich, who in western terms is similar to the Dalai Lama, has been in exile since 1966, while his Budhist teachings are also still banned in the state. The authorities suggested that he has neither applied to return through the proper channels, or through the official Buddhist organisation. (*Index* 6/1999). (*International Herald Tribune*)

ZAMBIA

Twelve journalists from the daily *Post* were summoned to court on 25 November, on charges of espionage, following an article which questioned the country's capacity to withstand an Angolan invasion. The case was adjourned until 22 December to allow the attendance of prosecution witnesses. (IPI)

Alponsius Hamachilla, reporter with the *Monitor* newspaper, was badly beaten by associates of the ruling Movement for Multi-Party Democracy (MMD) during the week of 14 November. Hamachilla had recently written an article that implied corruption, on the part of an MMD candidate at a by-election. (IPI)

ZIMBABWE

Christopher Mushowe, principal director in the office of President Mugabe, has begun a defamation suit against the now defunct *Sunday Gazette* over articles published in 1996. Mushowe is suing Modus Publications reporter **Basildon Peta** and university lecturer **John Makumbe** after the accusation that he fraudulently enrolled in a masters degree programme. (MISA)

Basildon Peta was also one of three reporters threatened in November, when he found three bullets in his mailbox along with a note reading, 'Watch out or you are dead'. **Ray Choto** (*Index* 3/1999, 4/1999, 6/1999), of the *Sunday Standard,* had two bullets and a child's toy delivered to his home, while **Ibbo Mandaza** of the *Zimbabwe Mirror* was threatened in a telephone call. (WAN)

Compiled by: Jake Barnes, Shifa Rahman, Daniel Rogers, François Vinsot (Africa); Rupert Clayton, Andrew Kendle, Jason Pym, Robin Tudge (Asia); Katy Sheppard (eastern Europe); Dolores Cortés, Daniel Rogers (south and central America); Arif Azad (Middle East); Humfrey Hunter (north America and Pacific); Steve Donachie (UK and western Europe). Edited by Simon Martin

Colombia: Homage to Jaime

Jaime Garzón's murder was the most shocking in a flood that has forced over one million people onto the terrified roads. Colombia is where the ancient feud between left and right intersects with the monetarised violence of a cocaine-based political economy. Torn between its citizens' appetite and the threat to security, Washington is worried. Standing above them all is the ultimate censor

File compiled by Michael Griffin, with Dolores Cortés

A blind man busking in Bogotoa – Credit: Paul Smith/Panos

MALCOLM DEAS

An empty horizon

Riven by rebels and now drugs, South America's longest-running democracy appears to teeter on the edge of fragmentation.

'The commonest cause of war is war.' – Alex de Waal, *Index 5/1999*

'Our moral engagements with faraway places are notoriously selective and partial.' – Michael Ignatieff, *The Warrior's Honour. Ethnic War and the Modern Conscience.*

I have in front of me a label from a coffee jar – Waitrose's Colombian Instant. In front of a botanically dubious grove of trees, where the artist has distributed some Mexican-hatted pickers, stands his idea of the owner, bearded and moustachioed. He wears an extravagant brass-buttoned and gold-embroidered coat with scarlet epaulettes, a sort of militarised smoking jacket, and holds a floral teacup and saucer. Of course, none of this is remotely like the real thing, but this Colombian scene is even less like the real thing than the general run of labels.

I have also made a (not exhaustive) list of six prominent and articulate Colombians I have known who have been assassinated in the last decade – three politicians, two academics and a comedian. The politicians are Luis Carlos Galán, Alvaro Gómez and Bernardo Jaramillo, the academics Jesús Antonio Bejarano and Darío Betancourt, and the comedian Jaime Garzón, Colombia's more intellectual Cantinflas. All quite different in their careers and allegiances and antecedents, all now censored by the ultimate censor. In two cases, perhaps three, there is evidence pointing to the drug trade but in not a single case can one be entirely sure who were the perpetrators. In two of the last three murders they could have been the paramilitaries or the guerrillas, and one could be just a common crime. More than one plausible account is possible, and one should also remind oneself that it is often impossible for a 'normal' imagination to conceive the reasoning processes of small, armed, clandestine and violent groups. The threats and the actions that silence people in Colombia come from many different directions, and may have motives at which one cannot guess.

Last November an estimated 2.5 million people in Bogotá demonstrated in the streets against violence – say a third of the city's population. Other cities have mounted demonstrations of similar proportion. The immediate effect of these marches on the various perpetrators of the violence that they are directed against is not so apparent – they may have some long-term impact on the more political elements in the guerrilla leadership, but they won't soften the harder hearts, those of the criminals often contracted by the political elements, or of those wedded to the armed struggle. Perhaps for that reason – their very lack of an easily definable point – the marches have been barely reported abroad; in this country news about them only reached insomniacs listening to the BBC World Service. Yet they are significant. They are monumental protests against violence: not in favour of the government, which stands low in the polls; not against or in favour of the military, though they stand rather higher; not in favour of guerrillas or paramilitaries, both even lower in the polls than the politicians; not in favour of peace at any price; not in favour of this or that reform; but against massacre, killing, kidnapping, disappearence, uprooting and all the manifestations of violence from which the country has so long suffered.

The label on the jar, the confusing list of dead, the massive unreported crowds ... Colombia is not all that far away from Europe or from the US, but our 'moral engagement' – or intellectual engagement for that matter – is as if with somewhere very far away indeed. It is as if a sort of censorship was at work. To a certain cast of mind one of the country's attractions has been that it is little known and little visited. It has not hitherto been a country that possesses the strategic interest that attracts journalists and academics, so the coverage has usually been 'selective and partial': drugs, homicide, massacre, paramilitaries and guerrillas, usually without context and with little recognition of the enormous harm that drugs have done the country, make up nearly all the erratic notice it receives in the UK press and media, with the honourable exceptions of the *Economist* and the *Financial Times*. It cannot be at all clear who is doing what to whom, and why, or what the country's prospects are. Here is a *tour d'horizon*, a version as dispassionate as I can make it.

Colombia is an aspiring democracy and has been for all but a few years of its 170 years of independent history. Its democratic record is, commonly, far too easily written off as a facade, dismissed as merely formal by those who adopt the rhetoric of local critics, but it is more than that. The electorate is part clientelistic, part opinion, as in a lot of other democracies better known. Politicians do respond to public opinion, and the system does produce some capable and courageous figures: Antanas Mockus, a recent elected Mayor of Bogotá, is a more interesting politician than any candidate currently on offer in London, and his achievements were not negligible. Some parts of the country are more democratic than others, but to govern you have to have votes, and elections are genuine and competitive. In areas of their sway, guerrillas have learnt not to oppose them; they impose promises on candidates, who must canvass to survive, and they manipulate those who are elected.

The country's problems do not stem from any lack of elections, from restrictions on liberty and participation imposed from above or from government curtailment of the conventional political freedoms. All the protagonists in Colombia's conflicts exploit the tolerant and frequently sensationalist local media as much as they can, even from inside jail. A Reuters television team recently obligingly filmed guerrilla military drill in prison in Bogotá, with easier access than even Northern Ireland's Maze prison. The limits on expression and political activity are those of prudence in the face of menace, limits real enough.

In the 1940s and 1950s competition for power between the republic's two traditional parties, Liberals and Conservatives, became sectarian and violent, and the first rural guerrillas emerged, mostly Liberal. By 1957, when the Liberals and Conservatives made a power-sharing agreement to end the sectarian fighting and oust a brief military government, most of the Liberal guerrillas, whose motivations were primarily partisan, had stopped fighting, but some continued under Communist influence. These, the original nucleus of the country's principal guerrilla movement the Fuerzas Armadas de la Revolución Colombiana (FARC), were encouraged by Castro's victory in Cuba, which also inspired the Ejército de Liberación Nacional (ELN), currently the second largest guerrilla organisation. Their activity, and violence in general, seemed to decline in the mid–1970s, when homicides fell to around 20 per 100,000, high enough but nowhere near the 70s and 80s of recent years.

Violence then began to increase again. The new resources for the armed movements came from drugs and from more intense extortion, particularly from the oil industry, and from kidnapping. Some new inspiration came from revolutionary events in Central America. Popular support was immaterial. Fronts were multiplied, 'presence' in municipalities spread wider, though the usual figures – 'one-third of the country', or more according to taste – do not convey that the guerrilla presence is concentrated in the more sparsely populated areas. The FARC may number some 20,000 under arms, some more militant than others, and the ELN some 7,000. In the 1980s a number of anti-guerrilla paramilitary groups emerged, whose ranks are now said to be around 5,000. The country's population is estimated at over 41 million.

With some lowering of the figures, a similar resumé could have been written 10 or even 20 years ago. Attempts to make peace have likewise been going on for a long time – the current series, initiated, frustrated and broken off as elected governments come and go every four years, should be dated back as far as the administration of President Julio César Turbay from 1978 to 1982. President Andrés Pastrana's efforts, novel in some aspects as they are, are only the most recent in a long line of intermittent negotiations. With some smaller groups they have even been successful.

History is essential, as essential to understanding Colombian guerrillas and paramilitaries as it is to understanding Northern Ireland, another intractable conflict with which we are more familiar, and one in some ways similar. The guerrilla leadership is as obsessed with history as any studious jailed Ulster paramilitary or provisional. A recent Bogotá publication has the attractive title *Las verdaderas intenciones de las FARC* (The Real Intentions of the FARC). One has to buy it, just in case it lives up to its promise, but it turns out to be nearly all history: the origins of the struggle, the official guerrilla version of who did what in the 1950s and 1960s. Not much of it is programme, project, policy. The conflict it contains is about the conflict; the cause of this war is war.

The FARC's achievement is its history, its survival, growth and its organisation, which is now primarily military and logistical, and still much embodied in its veteran leader Manuel Marulanda, active since the 1950s. It obviously needs a large income and has consequently acquired large interests. Figures vary about how much comes from taxing, encouraging and protecting the drug business; 38% is the lowest estimate I have seen, but such precision should have its pinch of salt and other estimates are much higher. The FARC always point out that they are not alone in making money out of this business. The movement's political pronouncements are sparse and uninteresting. It has a 10-point programme, last revised in 1992, but it is a tired and uninspired document to which nobody inside or outside the organisation, inside or outside the country, pays much attention. Colombian public opinion is always ready to criticise and there is therefore a lot to be said for not having much of a programme: if you don't have one, then it cannot be criticised.

So, as they say in the little book: 'We don't have much to negotiate.' The movement's stance in the current peace negotiations – and the ELN's is similar – is both to bring violent pressure to bear and to supervise and approve while the 'new Colombia' somehow emerges from a process of popular consultation. When 90% – their percentage, not mine – of the undefined new Colombia is in place, then they will consider stopping fighting. 'Decommisioning' is not even on the distant horizon.

There are many problems here and many hidden rationalities. The guerrillas do not have the moral authority or popular following to support the role they ascribe to themselves – some give the revolutionary's explanation that popularity comes after taking power, not before. The paramilitaries contest their pretensions violently, commonly by terrorising and expelling populations in areas deemed to be under guerrilla influence and a government that concedes too much in the guerrilla direction excites even more activity from the paramilitary quarter. Leaving aside the question of how much of the guerrilla leadership wishes to convert one sort of acquired capital, military, into another sort, political, those leaders who do are faced with the difficulty of imagining how to do so, and with the severe strains that any armed movement faces when making such a change, or even in agreeing to a truce.

Advance too fast, and you will be accused of betraying the movement, its history, its legacy, its dead. Discipline and morale depend to some degree on fighting, or at least on the prospect of it – as in most wars of this sort, for long periods in most places nothing much happens

– and both discipline and morale are difficult to maintain while hanging around in a truce. Resources come from drugs and extortion and kidnapping, this last being both a source of income in itself and the sanction that guarantees the flow from extortion. These are not peacetime activities; from where, in peace, will similar resources come? Some leaders have more political talents and prospects than others though, in general, political talent is rather thin. After so many years and so much history, distrust of the army is visceral and any change in the mode of political activity will obviously require elaborate and expensive guarantees.

The FARC will remind you of what happened to its political arm, the Unión Patriotica (UP), when in the mid-1980s it followed the impossible doctrine of 'the combination of all forms of struggle', peaceful and violent, into the electoral arena: a great many in the UP were killed. (The FARC will not remind you of the murkier aspects of that episode, which included rivalry and feud with drug interests, nor that the political dead at that time also included many representatives of other parties as well.) The guerrillas have lots of enemies, and many of them they deserve.

Though the guerrillas, like the army, continually exaggerate their military gains, they are not at present under much pressure to negotiate, and many are obviously quite happy to carry on.

How can an account of all this be dispassionate? Most writers, whatever they think they are doing, try to enlist sympathies – most for the non-combatant victims and the displaced, some for guerrillas, some against paramilitaries, some against outside intervention and pressure – criticising the nefarious US and its drug policies – some in favour of it – asserting that 'something should be done', seeking the benign attentions of the 'international community'.

What has to be done is to create a more effective state, which means better justice – in the most basic and old-fashioned, rather than social sense – and more effective forces of order, which means armed forces and police: in the last resort, what curtails paramilitaries and guerrilla warlords is state force.

Colombia does not have an authoritarian tradition and historically has had weak governments and skeletal administrative structures. The national penchant is to look for solutions in political deals, not in creating stronger institutions, for which the resources simply did not exist for most of the country's history. This tradition of weak government persisted even when greater resources became available, something along Italian lines: it is not poverty any more that accounts for the peculiarities of Italian government.

There have been some signs of progress and greater lucidity in these directions. A more effective state has to be created whether accords are reached among the combatants or not, as accords alone will not provide the necessary guarantees. A more effective state may bring such accords nearer. A human rights policy towards Colombia, in the US or in the EU, ought to have some prospect of improving the chances for human rights, and I doubt that that end is best attained by the pariah treatment some recommend, which might well make matters worse. Without a more effective state those who try to do something, as in their different ways did all the six on my list, will go on risking their lives. ❏

Malcom Deas *is a fellow of St Antony's, Oxford and co-founder of the University's Latin American Centre. His essays have been included in* Del Poder y La Grammatica *(Taurus),* Intercambios Violentes *(Alfaguara) and* The Legitimisation of Violence *(Macmillan, 1997). He first visited Colombia in 1963*

ANONYMOUS

The fingers pointing

'We *campesinos* are not violent, we don't carry arms. At most a shotgun for hunting. We want to work and bring up our children. In the country we got on with our own business but, here in the town of Riosucio, all we do is eat *platanos* and watch the people go by. And the days do get long.

The children want everything they see – t–shirts, clothes, shoes. And one hasn't any money. Not like in the country. There they don't want anything, they are happy with the animals, the river, the work. It was hard having to leave the settlement. We'd made a big investment in organising the plots and building the houses. It's very painful to leave what has taken years of effort, and the more so because people had already lost land in other parts in the previous violence. Many have been always on the move, defenceless people fleeing from bullying and bullets.

The government gets annoyed when they kill soldiers in these zones where there is conflict, but we are not responsible. It hurts us to see any of the combatants killed. They're all just people, people's relations, people you know or people from elsewhere who all end up involved in a war that has no sense.

The army only appeared in the Atrato villages at election time, when the candidates needed protection. So the guerrilla had all the time in the world to get a hold on those parts. It is like when one goes walking along the river and fishing, walking and fishing, further and further, so one knows where one can get food and not run any risks. That's the way the subversion advanced.

We are poor here but we have lived well, even in the last years when the guerrillas laid down the law. Until the paramilitaries and the army came. The guerrillas, the *muchachos*, they let you work. I never had to give them part of the harvest. But the problem now is contact; because guerrilla vengeance has begun. They say the peasants betray them.

Many of us left for Riosucio. The guerrillas said we were turning our backs on them, because we were in the area of the paramilitaries. We have to speak with the soldiers to find out what is going to happen, and then we pay the price for that too. The guerrillas and the paramilitaries watch each other at a distance, but they always come for us as if we were the only ones responsible for what happens. We can't go back to our lands because we run the danger they will kill us. They can go where they like, they destroy and move on. For a *campesino*, it's different: the land is one's life.

With us moving out like this, our children don't have any example in anything. One wants them to study and to work, but they don't let them. They try to turn them into combatants. Some join the guerrillas and some the paramilitaries. If one group doesn't persecute them, the other will. We go round in circles trying to work out which is best: paramilitaries, guerrillas or army. In reality none of them is any good, because they are here today and gone tomorrow and they molest and the *campesino* is in the middle of the shooting and the fingers pointing.

What would be good would be that in this zone there would remain the civil authorities of the government and our own – the community and *campesino* organisations. But the *armados* want things only one way. It's as if there was just one bottle between them: now I want it, now the other wants it – each one wants to do something different with it, each wants it just for himself. I want it for everyone, for us.' ❑

Students at the National University of Colombia in Bogota. The graffiti shows a chainsaw, the favoured terror weapon of the paramilitaries –
Credit: Phillip Jones Griffiths/Magnum

The speaker is a displaced person in Riosucio, Chocó department, interviewed in 1997. From Relatos e imágines: el desplazamiento en Colombia *(CINEP, Bogotá, 1997), by Carlos Alberto Giraldo, Jesus Abad Colorado and Diego Pérez*

AMANDA ROMERO

Euphemisms that kill

Abrir(se) (To open up): To walk away, to leave someone behind
Arrancar(se) (To snatch): To flee
Bajar (To go down): To kill, to murder
Boleteo: To extort, to threaten to kill someone
Caleta: Place where weapons, cocaine or other illegal objects are stashed
Cambuche: Guerrillas' hiding place; place where hostages are kept.
Campanero: A lookout
Cazarretenes: New US-trained army 'elite force'
Chicharrón (Pork crackling): A situation or person that brings about state repression
Chusma (Rabble): Guerrilla, militia
Cirugía (Surgery): A form of killing whereby a victim's stomach is cut open, filled with stones and sewn up
Corte de corbata (Necktie cut): The victim is beheaded, his tongue is cut off and then placed on the torso to resemble a tie
Dar papaya (To give [a] papaya): To cause a situation where harm is likely to occur
Dar(le) (To give (him or her)): To kill or wound someone
Desechable (Throwaway): A person considered 'useless' or a threat who has been targeted by death squads
Donación (Donation): Money paid as a result of extortion or in exchange for hostages
Duro (Hard, strong): A powerful or rich person, a leader or boss
Fumigar (To fumigate): To kill, to systematically and indiscriminately eliminate real or supposed opponents
Guerreros (Warriors, War-makers): Guerrillas
Lapidar (To stone): To kill, to threaten to kill
Limpiar (To clean): To kill systematically or indiscriminately

Llevar la lápida al cuello (To wear a headstone around one's neck): To risk being killed following death threats

Marcar calavera (To look like a skeleton): To be very close to death or on a death list

Merca (from '*mercancía*', merchandise): Cocaine

Motosierra (Electric saw): A form of killing that involves the use of electric saws to cut up victims

Muchachos (Kids): Guerrillas

Paila: A person likely to be assassinated – or in financial difficulties

Para or Paraco: A member of the death squads, paramilitary groups or 'self-defence' groups

Parasubversivo (also '*paraguerrilleros*'): A paramilitary term to designate NGO workers, academics or intellectuals whom they accuse of collaborating with guerrillas

Patiamarrados: Members of the armed forces (guerrilla slang)

Payaso (Clown): An official informer, paid by the state

Pazólogo(a) (Peaceologist): Academic who studies the peace process

Pesca Milagrosa (Miraculous catch [of fish]): A large-scale kidnapping

Pisar(se) (To step on): To flee

Quebrar (To break): To kill or murder

Raqueta: Requisition, (also burglary)

Raspachín: A coca leaf cultivator.

Retención: The capture of soldiers, police or civilians by guerrillas

Sapo (Toad): A traitor, informer

Sicario: A mercenary

Sufragio (Suffrage): Condolences sent to the victim, indicating the day and hour of his or her execution

Tartamuda (stammerer): Machine gun

Tira: Undercover intelligence police officer

Traqueto: Assassin who prefers a machine gun. A cocaine middleman

Tumbar (To knock down): To steal

Vacuna (Vaccine): Extortion quota paid by landowners, merchants and the rich to the guerrillas

Violentología (Violentology): Academic discipline concerned with the study of violence in its many guises in Colombia ❏

Amanda Romero *is a human rights researcher based in Bogotá. Translated by Paulo Drinot*

FABIO CASTILLO

The unpublished war

With the media dominated by two conglomerates, Colombians aren't getting their full quota of news

When a war-weary Colombian listens to a news story on the radio or television he or she is drawn into another battle: the information battle. This battle is fought not by journalists, but by the two most powerful economic groups in the country – the Santodomingo Group and the Ardila Lulle Group.

Media ownership is highly concentrated. Five out of every 10 news stories are generated by the Santodomingo group, four out of 10 by the Ardila Lulle group. Only one out of 10 stories is from any other source.

Santodomingo and Ardila Lulle are not just media conglomerates. Their interests include manufacturing, banking and commerce and their radio and television stations carry the bulk of their companies' advertising. Money thus circulates within the corporations. Now that the two groups have signed an agreement that lets them advertise on each other's television stations, money also circulates between them.

In November 1998, Francisco Santos, *El Tiempo*'s press officer, noted: 'Much as OPEC fixes production quotas to raise or lower the price of oil, the Ardila and Santodomingo groups agreed to advertise on each others' channels. They thus created a television cartel not unlike the oil cartels, and will have to face the dangers that any cartel faces'.

This statement coincided with the signing of the groups' advertising agreement, which came hot on the heels of their successful bids for the first two private television channels in Colombia. The groups competed openly for the television channels, but the level of the bidding (US$95 million) made it practically impossible for anyone else to take part.

The franchises were awarded during the Ernesto Samper Pizano administration of 1994-98. At the time, President Samper was under great international pressure, having been accused of receiving US$6 million from the Rodríguez Orejuela drug cartel during his election campaign. The Ardila and Santodomingo groups were members of a business lobby known as *Los Cacaos* (an expression that in football terms translates as 'those who own the ball'). Today it is widely acknowledged that *Los Cacaos*'s support was crucial for Samper at a time when public opinion at home and abroad favoured his resignation.

There are 1,200 radio stations in Colombia. Thanks to the Caracol (Santodomingo) and RCN (Ardila) radio networks, the two leading groups control 50% of radio stations, either outright or as affiliates. Naturally, they also control the bulk of advertising. Some estimates give Caracol and RCN control 50% and 45% of radio advertising respectively. The rest is shared by a hundred or so stations, such as Todelar, Radio Santafé or Super, whose independence is their main selling point.

According to the state pollster Dane, 89% of Colombians get their news from television but 72.3% also hear it on the radio. As a result journalism has become highly dependent on the advertising revenue the big groups pull in. This produces an information bottleneck with only two sources to turn to for news. These sources do not always provide news that matches the needs of Colombians. More importantly, the dominant media positions of the Santodomingo and Ardila groups are an obstacle to the spread of alternative viewpoints.

Since President Andrés Pastrana's election in 1998 the government has been engaged in peace talks with the FARC, ELN and the ELP guerrilla groups. In what amounts to an undeclared war that has lasted for half a century, these groups (comprising some 25,000 armed men in total) seek to take over the country. In early December 1999, the FARC agreed to talk with the directors of the main media groups on the 'misinformation' surrounding the main aspects of the peace process. According to the guerrillas, news stories are usually pro-establishment. Little mention is made, the guerrillas argue, of the important steps that they have taken as part of the continuing dialogue.

Santodomingo's interests are not restricted to television and radio. The group purchased *El Espectador*, once the most influential newspaper in Colombia. Guillermo Cano Isaza, *El Espectador*'s former director, was gunned down outside his office building 10 years ago after leading some

INDEX ON CENSORSHIP 1 2000   129

of the most important battles against political corruption and drug cartels as well as being an ardent supporter of human rights.

However, *El Espectador* has not succeeded in regaining its previous levels of credibility under Santodomingo. For one thing, it carried stories with the express purpose of defending certain economic interests: the launch of a new beer was camouflaged as a news story. Everyone knew that Santodomingo had been involved in Samper's defence. It then installed Rodrigo Pardo, Samper's ex-foreign minister, as director along with Ramiro Bejarano, a former chief of the secret police, and Alvaro Uribe Vélez, an ex-governor of Antioquia thought to have links to the paramilitaries. Naturally, *El Tiempo* benefited. In 1998, *El Espectador* ran a deficit of US$17 million and this is likely to have grown in 1999.

El Tiempo boasts a readership and influence twice as large as that of *El Espectador*. Under its present directors, the veteran journalists Enrique Santos Calderón and Rafael Santos, the paper has achieved levels of independence undreamed of five years ago. But *El Tiempo* is at the heart of another media conglomerate, almost as powerful as the other two, which includes the Sarmiento Angulo Organisation and Antioquia Syndicate among its members. It owns a local television station, CityTV, and a network of weekly regional papers.

The *El Tiempo* group (CEET) faces competition from a second network of regional newspapers, organised around Bucaramanga's *Vanguardia Liberal*. This newspaper controls seven newspapers in as many cities, as well as a pay-per-view television network, and is a partner of another similar network. Following the launch by CEET of *Portafolio*, the most ambitious project in financial journalism in the country, two other influential newspapers, *El Colombiano* from Medellín and *La República* from Bogotá, a financial newspaper, struck an alliance.

Faced with this concentration of ownership, most journalists opt for self-censorship. Journalists invoke the old adage: 'the goal of journalism is to make friends, not enemies'. One example of this came to light following the purchase of *El Espectador*. To avoid a salary war that would have raised journalists' wages, the companies agreed not to hire journalists from other newspapers. The arrangement did not apply to radio, where agreements (rather than contracts) are common. Radio journalists often sell advertising spots in order to raise their salaries. The only way to obtain adverts is through the companies themselves, which further reduces journalists' independence.

To make matters worse, media companies rarely sign a contract with journalists. Usually journalists sign civil contracts or are paid on a piecework basis, thus foregoing social security benefits. For this, journalists put their lives at risk. More than 60 have been killed in the last 20 years. In most cases, those responsible have not been brought to justice. Yet everyone knows who they are: angry politicians, mafias organised around cocaine and corruption, right-wing groups that confuse alternative viewpoints with pro-guerrilla sentiments.

During the week I wrote this piece, a bomb was thrown at the Cali offices of *El Tiempo*, a cameraman and a photographer were assassinated by a paramilitary organisation and a cameraman died during a guerrilla operation in the south of the country. In addition, a Reuters photographer was freed by the ELN following a 'trial' for having photographed a guerrilla who had taken off his hood.

According to Albert Camus, journalism is the most beautiful profession on earth. In Colombia it is the most dangerous. However, against all the odds, an alternative press is beginning to make itself heard. Already there are some 500 community-based radio or television stations in different regions of the country. The prohibition against carrying advertising has hampered their growth, but these stations are already seen as authentic spokespeople for local concerns.

Like the *Revista Alternativa*, the independent monthly magazine I edit, these initiatives seek to challenge information that emanates from a single sourcel. We recently investigated Enrique Penalosa Londóno, the mayor of Bogotá, who has invested US$65 million in advertising. No media group has dared to publish the fact that a group, largely consisting of Penalosa's relatives and former business partners, also handle a large part of Bogotá's budget. *Revista Alternativa* detailed all the companies involved. Hardly any radio or television channel picked up the story. Nor did Javier Baena, president of *El Espectador* and executive of another Bogotá company. *El Tiempo* published a brief synopsis. The mayor threatened to sue, but backed down. Thereafter, Penalosa began a publicity campaign, and nothing more was said. The mayor had bought off the Bogotá press. ❑

Fabio Castillo *is co-director and editor of Bogotá's* Revista Alternativa. *This year Human Rights Watch awarded him the Hellman-Hammet Grant. Translated by Paulo Drinot*

JAIME GARZON

They shoot comedians

Garzón is dressed as the kitchen maid of Government Palace. There is a party attended by '*Tirofijo*'[FARC commander], who is playing cards. President Andrés Pastrana is talking to US ambassador Myles Frechette. He taunts Frechette with a riddle:

'It is white, Colombia makes it and gringos eat it.'

Frechette answers: 'It must be salt.'

Pastrana: 'No, it is not salt.'

Frechette: 'If it is not salt, then it must be the coco [nut].'

The maid says: 'Yes, yes, it's the coco, that little magic powder we are always talking about.

An advert for ELN guerrillas directed at the small investor. Voiceover: 'Worried about your money? Relax, you no longer have to worry about money. Invest your savings in official certificates. ELNs are the only market instruments that can convert a heap of oil into a mountain of money. Remember that nefarious liquid emissions are not taxable or subject to deductions at source. There's no time to waste, invest now in nefarious liquid emissions. Your future will be like oil: black.'

A woman looking out her window sees the Rodríguez family [drug cartel] leaving their apartment block. The family is wanted by the police. She calls the police. The captain regretfully informs her that the Rodríguez family does not exist, he has checked the phonebook and there is no Rodríguez family listed. The woman perseveres:

'I've spent the last 25 minutes trying to hand you these bad men. Now they are leaving. They're getting into a car with some politicians. God! These politicians are like Pontius Pilate, some denied him and others wash their hands of him. But captain, if you come quickly you'll understand what is happening in this country. Too late, they're gone. I'll call you again next week.' ❏

Edited transripts of television satires by journalist and humourist **Jaime Garzón** *(1995). At 6am on 13 August, Garzón was executed on his way to the Radionet studio by two men riding on a motorcycle. Garzón, known for his intervention in the stalled peace process, had reportedly been threatened by Carlos Castaño, head of the paramilitary United Self-Defence Force of Colombia (AUC), in the preceding days. According to colleagues, Garzón planned to meet Castaño on 14 August. The AUC denied any responsibility in the assassination. Translated by Paulo Drinot*

OSCAR COLLAZOS

Funeral of laughter

**'They have murdered laughter', cried Colombians as they
mourned the buffoon who told insolent truths to the world**

Jaime Garzón was a popular comedian. He made his name in
television, though of course his ratings were never as high as those of
Colombian soap operas. It took him less than 10 years to become a
celebrity. He owed his fame to artful mimicry, to his biting criticism of
politicians, media pundits and celebrities and to the characters he
created, adept caricatures of presidents, ministers, congressmen,
diplomats, journalist and actresses.

His popularity was such that he could easily have made a bid for the
presidency, like Coluche in France. Yet Jaime Garzón was popular for a
more profound reason. No one really knew whether he upset those he
imitated or whether they thanked him for making them twice as famous:
for who they were and for Garzón's faultless imitations.

Garzón became so popular that he was routinely invited round to the
houses of his 'victims'. His love affairs, real or imagined, and his capacity
to be in all places at all times with the 'right' people turned him into a
news item. Despite his humble beginnings and his enduring ugliness, he
now made more money than most comedians could dream of and was
toasted by the jet set.

After making his debut on the *Zoociedad* (Zoo-society) programme,
he spent nine years honing his comic skills. His last character, Heriberto
de la Calle, was a cheeky, dirty and toothless shoeshine. Heriberto de la
Calle, a wordplay on the names of a former Colombian president and of
the current British ambassador, abused the politicians and celebrities he
interviewed, thus endearing Garzón to large segments of the audience.

But there was another Garzón. The comedian who poked fun at
guerrilla leaders and the military high command worked tirelessly as a
mediator to free those kidnapped by the guerrillas. This is the most

Jaime Garzón – Credit: Orlano Cuellar

probable cause of his assassination. Loved by all Colombians, Garzón was a resourceful and intelligent buffoon who became a successful negotiator just as the war turned sour. Who benefited from the assassination? The war itself, of course, and its armed protagonists (the military high command, the guerrillas and the paramilitaries).

Shortly after his death, the spot where Garzón was assassinated, near the radio station where he worked every morning, was turned into a shrine. This was an absurd murder. Across Colombia, indignation soon spilled over into the streets as people started to mourn the buffoon who told insolent truths to the world. 'They have murdered laughter' became the rallying cry of journalists and Colombians in general who protested at Garzón's assassination.

On the day of the funeral, this cry resonated through the streets of Bogotá, as mourners made their way to the cemetery. Ironically, Garzón was to be buried in the Gardens of Peace of a country at war for half a century. A bridge brimming over with mourners and onlookers collapsed, and another unfortunate soul became Garzón's travelling companion as the comedian set off for purgatory – it being understood that neither hell nor heaven is a suitable place for a buffoon.

Thousands of Colombians mourned Garzón as they would a lifelong friend. Many thought that he would have laughed at the homage. With reason: the comedian's funeral had become a national tragedy. Garzón thus became yet another victim–turned–martyr of Colombia's violence. His murder was called a 'magnicide'. All those he poked fun at mourned him: the president, ex-presidents, the military and the police.

Garzon had been a friendly enemy: he never shunned the establishment. He welcomed them into his home. Perhaps they needed to clear their consciences. The fact that they mourned an anarchist is proof that their grief was not sincere. They mourned a media event. By contrast, the grief of most Colombians was authentic, as was that of Garzón's close friends and of journalists.

The beautiful women who had sought his company mourned him. It is well known that women love men who can make them laugh. Yet because he had become a media item, Garzón was also mourned by those he had made the butt of his jokes. ❏

Oscar Collazos is a novelist, a columnist for El Tiempo *newspaper and a correspondant for* Vanguardia *in Spain. Translated by Paulo Drinot*

ALVARO MONTOYA GOMEZ

I drown in silence

Any serious journalist in Colombia faces a constant struggle to overcome threats and intimidation – the struggle can end in two ways, one of which is to stop kicking and sink beneath the waves

I learnt from Rabindranath Tagore that a person must do all in his or her power to remain afloat. When this is no longer possible he or she should drown in silence.

I have followed the great Indian poet's advice throughout my career as a journalist, and not without success. Doctor Alvaro Gómez convinced me that journalism was the appropriate career for someone with a penchant for telling the world what he thinks. I have done what I could to remain afloat through this column for the last two decades and through my cartoons for the past five years.

These are my favourite variants of op-ed journalism. They have given me the greatest personal satisfaction. Gómez taught me two basic things about journalism: that journalism without freedom is impossible and that every day we fight for freedom through these columns and cartoons. I am unable to renounce these beliefs in order to continue working. I feel gratified to have been given a space in which to make my opinions known, either as text or cartoons.

Three weeks ago, on the fourth anniversary of Doctor Gómez's assassination, my children received the most serious threats so far. I could no longer brush them off as 'occupational hazards'. I could no longer shield my loved ones from these threats. They produced a state of fear in my family that served to heighten their severity.

I found myself in an intolerable position: besieged by some members of my family and morally kidnapped by the vile authors of the threats. This sudden disruption to my home's tranquility has robbed me of the freedom without which I am unable to write or draw.

I do not know for how long I will refrain from making my opinions known. I do know that that both the Bionaut and Alfin know that I am inspired by a noble if selfish cause, and that they will understand, as will, I hope, my readers, friends and colleagues.

I did all I could to remain afloat but, as I can no longer do so, I drown in silence.

Some final opinions: I am incapable of euphemism. I cannot be a light journalist. When I am forbidden to write about a subject, all other subjects become off-bounds. If I am not allowed to write freely, it is better not to do it all. I prefer silence to silences. ❏

Alvaro Montoya Gomez *wrote a weekly column, 'Notes from a Bionaut', for the magazine* El Nuevo Siglo *until 25 November when he was forced to abandon it after death threats against his family. He has also given up working as a cartoonist, which he practised under the pseudonym Alfin.*
Translated by Paulo Drinot

ROBIN KIRK

Pleasure and the digital war

Colombia faces a mortal paradox. The only products developed countries pay well for are cocaine and heroin, but the best client punishes it for supplying precisely what its consumers demand

A friend once told me that Colombian politics were complicated, but not confused. The opposite could be said for US policy in Colombia, which is confused, but deadly simple.

What is at stake is pleasure, not politics. Americans buy narcotics in record amounts, but we are ashamed of what we see as a rot at our cultural core. Blame the work ethic, whose reward is pleasure without limits. Or our Puritan heritage, TV, boredom. That's the confused part.

The result is that, even as we buy drugs, we make them illegal. President Richard Nixon was first to declare a 'war' on these drugs. Over the next three decades, the US public spent billions buying them and then billions more punishing the people who sell them. The resulting crime has prompted us to arm ourselves as no nation before in peacetime. Yet illegal drugs are cheaper, more potent, as easily available and as popular as ever.

Elections loom and the drug war has again edged on to the Teleprompters. No candidate acknowledges the astonishing failure of the 'war on drugs'. Being tough on drugs is a political necessity – like kissing babies. Republicans and Democrats share the view encapsulated by Al Gore: cocaine and heroin are on the wrong side of the 'fundamental line between right and wrong in our own minds and hearts'.

First-time visitors to Washington are often surprised to see that Congress is run by twenty-somethings. While the elected members, as they are known, pronounce on C-SPAN, their aides wrangle policy in offices that could double as college dormitory rooms. The 'war on drugs' was designed in such rooms. Like me, these aides were raised in a stew of recreational stimulants. But like Nixon and his successors, they place the blame for drugs not on users, but where it causes the least domestic turmoil: 'Over There'.

The Over There that matters most now is Colombia, which produces most of the cocaine and heroin sold in the US. Colombian traffickers dominate the distribution networks and are imaginative shippers, but Colombia has little choice. The global marketplace wants no more of its coffee, cattle or bananas. As Spanish sociologist Manuel Castells has written, the 'cyber-empires' need little from the likes of Colombia. One of the few ways left to engage is through crime: Castells calls it the 'perverse connection'. Russian mafias have made new ties to Colombia because Russia faces the same digital wall. The port of Turbo, which faces across the Caribbean at Florida, is favoured by Russian ships, which offload AK-47s in exchange for drugs.

The centrepiece of the US war on drugs is aerial eradication. Between 1990 and 1998, over US$1 billion in US assistance went to support the police in spraying the country's south. Aerial eradication is delightfully modern. It relies on machines and avoids troublesome human confrontation, unlike in the 1980s when Peruvians paid by the US to rip up coca bushes were shot by the irate neighbours and friends who farmed them. In Colombia, State Department pilots lay down Round Up pesticide in the morning and can be back in time for cocktails, without touching toe to ground. It's Kosovo, with corn and beans as the only collateral damage. I visited San José del Guaviare from where these flights originate. The US trainers looked more like software hackers than warriors. Their screens flickered with the arced paths of Turbo Thrushes going to fields scheduled for destruction that day.

Eradication has long had bipartisan support: Clinton authorised the first flight in 1994. When Republicans won the House, a half-dozen congressmen commandeered the issue as a way to bash the Clinton administration or, as one aide called it, 'the pot-smoking, cocaine-sniffing, heroin-snorting *Clintonistas*'. Among the most powerful is Dennis Hastert (R–IL), a former wrestling coach who became Speaker after Newt Gingrich and Bob Livingston were felled by financial and sexual peccadillos. The one with real gravitas, however, is Benjamin

Gilman (R–NY), a 27-year veteran and chair of the powerful House International Relations Committee. Gilman has repeatedly summoned administration officials before his committee to lambast them about Clinton's 'soft on drugs' policy. Officials dutifully countered with their own stacks of statistics. It seemed at times that the most prominent product of the drug war was these statistics, bound and collated in report after stultifying report. By 1999, anyone with a pen and paper could see that the US was losing, and losing dramatically.

The day I visited San José del Guaviare, the pilots were grounded by rain. The fields had been sprayed repeatedly, but the 'damn plants refused to die', said Pete, the boss. Pete wanted to go further out, but it was too far for the helicopters. Traffickers knew that the helicopter escorts had a two-hour radius, so they just planted beyond range. When the Turbo Thrushes went alone, pilots risked getting shot.

But more than simple logistics dooms eradication. Since the US began spraying, coca cultivation has nearly doubled from 67,200 hectares in 1996 to 101,800 in 1999 and is still rising. That may be the direct result of US policy. In the late 1980s, the US cut the air routes that fed Peruvian and Bolivian coca to Colombian laboratories for refinement. Instead of giving up, traffickers planted in the states of Caquetá and Putumayo, and opened new areas along the border with Venezuela.

But what of the arrests of the kingpins, the sensational death of Pablo Escobar and the imprisonment of the Cali cartel leaders? The removal of one trafficker has repeatedly meant that another steps in. In 1997, the Drug Enforcement Agency (DEA) reported that men from the state of Valle del Cauca had replaced the jailed leaders of the Cali cartel, who had themselves replaced Escobar. Business is booming. The finance ministry estimates that in 1998 narcotics brought in between US$3 billion and US$5 billion a year, making it the country's top earner.

The shift of coca to local turf prompted another development – the relationship between the drug trade and Colombia's irregular armies. When I visited in 1992, the Revolutionary Armed Forces of Colombia (FARC) in Putumayo enforced laws and meted out punishment. Just as guerrillas had 'taxed' cattle ranchers and oil drillers, once coca moved in, it too was 'taxed'. The FARC and the smaller National Liberation Army (ELN) make millions out of drugs but it is clear that they invest the money in war. In an analogous way, the paramilitaries also profit from drugs. With the acquiescence and, at times, open support of the army, they control much of the north where drugs are refined and packed for shipment. They sell protection to business people, cattle ranchers and landowners, often traffickers who have invested their fortunes in real estate. Last year, the DEA named Carlos Castaño, Colombia's main paramilitary leader, as a trafficker in his own right.

The resulting war has converted Colombia into what one observer calls an 'archipelago of bloody little independent republics'. In 1998 alone, the authorities recorded 194 massacres carried out for political reasons, outstripping even Algeria. More than 1.5 million people are internal refugees, double the number of Albanian Kosovars who fled Serbs at the peak of their terror. The 'war on drugs' has not only failed against narcotics, it has pushed Colombia to the brink of dissolution.

It took a loose cannon to blast the Washington stalemate. General (ret.) Barry McCaffrey, Clinton's drug policy adviser, returned from Colombia in 1999 like a millennial prophet. 'Colombia,' he intoned, 'is in a near-crisis situation.' He proposed a billion-dollar aid package to 'support the Colombian government in it attempts to reassert democratic control'. A look at McCaffrey's plan shows that far from strengthening democracy, what is proposed is more eradication. It will be 'ramped up' – Washington's lingo for opening the floodgates of military aid. Unfortunately for Colombia, that is just what most Americans want. A 1998 survey by the Harvard School of Public Health found that, while most Americans agree that US anti-drug efforts have failed, they support greater resources for these same efforts. Eighty-six per cent believed that more money should be spent on attacking drugs 'at the source'.

The bill's other innovation is that for the first time it pulls Colombia's abusive military into the drug war. McCaffrey argues that its criminal past is history, a conclusion disputed by human rights groups. Fresh from US training and equipped with the latest weaponry, the theory goes, the military will vanquish the 'narco-guerrilla' threat. US policy-makers appear to have swallowed whole the criminal logic of the Colombian military. Paramilitaries are considered responsible for 78% of the human rights violations, but the army steers clear of trying to pursue them.

Certainly, the potion is assisted by the rotting whiff of Cold War rhetoric, which Colombia's brass continues to embrace. In most official drug war literature, it is possible to replace the words 'war on drugs', 'cocaine' and 'heroin' with 'war on communism', 'communists' and 'subversives', allowing veteran managers in Washington to continue justifying their salaries with portents of the next battle for the American soul. I don't agree with the theory of a dark conspiracy, a US plot to invade and rule Colombia from Imperial DC. Rather, I think a lack of imagination is at the root, a somatic inability to accept the fall of the Wall and the new realities it has created.

Americans lack the stomach for direct intervention. They prefer cyber-wars like Kosovo. The crash of a US Army RC-7B DeHavilland intelligence-gathering aircraft over the department of Putumayo in July underscored the already increased US involvement in Colombia's war, but it also sent a tremor through the Capitol. One of the five Americans killed was 29-year-old pilot Captain Jennifer Odom. Her husband, also an army officer, told reporters: 'American citizens would not support any involvement in any country that is going to cost American lives.'

Despite the war drums and Cold War rhetoric, the 106th Congress adjourned in November without approving an extra penny for Colombia. The Clinton administration said it was less important than the Wye Accords, overdue fees at the UN and a thousand and one pork projects for the folks at home. Money remains on the table. But as the election year begins in earnest, Colombia may fall by the wayside yet again. Governor George W. Bush and Vice-President Al Gore are positioning to find the most mediagenic way to blame each other for having 'lost' Colombia. What is crucial is that if Colombia is lost, the blame must be firmly laid at the doorstep of a political enemy.

Colombia faces a mortal paradox. The only products developed countries pay well for are cocaine and heroin, yet Colombia's best clients punish it for providing exactly what they demand. Meanwhile, drug profits fill the war chests of its armies. Which is to say that, far from subsiding, this war is likely to intensify. As an aide explained, the Democrats and Republicans agree the peace process is fatally flawed and the American public wants to see action – but not necessarily results – on drugs. 'The best way to do that is to say you are going to send money, lots of money.'

What happens to the money may be entirely beside the point. ❏

Robin Kirk is the author of The Monkey's Paw: New Chronicles from Peru *and a co-editor of* The Peru Reader: History, Culture, Politics. *She covers Colombia for Human Rights Watch. The views expressed here are the author's and do not reflect the views of Human Rights Watch*

STEVE DUDLEY

The real solution

Rather than tackling them at the root, the government is throwing money at Colombia's problems

It was a typical Colombian strike. The protesters covered their faces with scarves, bandannas and T-shirts and stood defiantly in the middle of the Pan-American highway. Then the self-appointed leader, simply identified as 'a farmer' by the local news, got a chance to explain the protestors' side of the problem.

'We are wondering when the government is going to start taking us seriously,' he said.

Newscasters made little mention of why 50,000 'farmers' had blocked the highway for two weeks or the government's response to their demand for US$240 million to alleviate the economic crisis in the region. The government was angry, they reported, because the farmers did not show up to the negotiations on time. 'Guerrillas' had infiltrated the ranks to sabotage the talks, an official said.

It was not long before the complexity of the situation in the south-eastern states of Cauca and Narino was lost in a sea of accusation. On the surface were small farmers seeking solutions to a deep-seated agricultural crisis that has left them without the means to produce the beans, corn, potatoes, and onions that make up their livelihood and diet. But behind the coverage was the economic depravity that powers Colombia's drug trade.

The government was supposed to follow up on anti-drugs programmes with economic packages, the most important of which are crop-substitution programmes. But these have failed throughout Colombia and will continue to fail unless changes are made.

Ricardo Vargas, who writes extensively on the drugs trade, claims the government has wasted over US$50 million on crop substitution. Some failed due to poor feasibility studies; others because the farmers used their credits to plant the legal substitute, while clearing new areas for a fresh batch of coca. But the deteriorating economy, with close to 20% unemployment, provided fertile ground for the failure. 'The coca grower knows that this government doesn't present real alterantives,' said Vargas. 'And that he has in his hands the means to resolve his problems: coca.'

An injection of US$289 million from the US this year has led to a regeneration of the very same programmes. Washington's emphasis remains firmly on fumigation: the US Agency for International Development has allocated just US$15 million to the government development agency PLANTE this year. Part will go towards crop substitution programmes for opium growers in Cauca and Narino.

Another programme tries to address the seemingly uncontrollable political element: the FARC. With the UN, the government is running a US$6 million scheme in the 42,000km² 'demilitarised' zone. The FARC could play a critical role in implementing a sustainable crop substitution programme for the guerrillas have political and military leverage in areas where the government does not. But the rebels do not have a clear handle on the depth of the problem and it is not part of their current agenda. 'The FARC is concerned with controlling territory,' Vargas said. 'To them the question of drugs is money.'

In Cauca and Narino, the government countered the protesting farmers' US$240 million demand with an US$40 million proposal of their own. But in the end, the US$200 million gap between them is but a gully compared to the chasm that exists between the proposed solution and real one. ❏

Steve Dudley *is a freelance reporter for National Public Radio, the BBC, the* Nation *and* In These Times. *He has lived in Bogotá since 1995*

EDUARDO PIZARRO LEONGOMEZ

Fashioning the peace

The FARC appears to control the direction of the new peace process but there is a fast-growing international dimension

The peace process was a key issue in the debates between presidential candidates in the 1998 electoral campaign. Horacio Serpa Uribe, the Liberal Party candidate, seemed best placed on the issue of peace, until the FARC secretariat announced that it favoured Andrés Pastrana, the Conservative Party candidate. This had wide-ranging repercussions and influenced the outcome of the elections, which Pastrana won.

A few days after the vote, Pastrana met the top FARC commander Manuel Marulanda Vélez, otherwise known as *'Tirofijo'* or 'Sure Shot'. This meeting led to a new round of the peace negotiations, which had been stalled for seven years. A number of factors account for the renewal of negotiations, but the change of government and the steps taken by the newly elected president were the most important.

No one would dispute the sincerity of the new government's attempts to end the conflict. Yet the peace process has had several mishaps. The government team in charge of negotiations has made a series of blunders. Similarly, a numbers of actions (ambushes, attacks on the economic infrastructure) have raised doubts over the guerrillas' real intentions. That these incidents have not killed off the peace process is largely due to the highly favourable context in which the negotiations are taking place.

Public opinion is seriously concerned about the grey areas that mar the peace process, however. Agreement has been reached on the main issues but several others are subject to different and conflicting interpretations.

There are two divergent interpretations of the possible ramifications of the negotiations in the 'demilitarised zones' in Meta and Caquetá departments from which the army withdrew in December 1998 as a pre-condition for talks with the FARC. The government views these talks as a step towards accords that will be ratified by a Constituent Assembly or by referendum. The FARC, meanwhile, believe the accords will be law.

There are also concerns about the dynamics of the accords. If the aim of the talks is to produce accords, then once the procedural obstacles are overcome, the peace process should proceed. But if the talks are to result in the immediate implementation of the accords, the peace process could have perverse consequences.

In fact, this has already happened. The FARC have tried to act as ad hoc 'observers' of the peace process, with the power to veto political decisions. As such they have controlled the pace and character of the peace process. Recently, the FARC secretariat has based its participation on its approval of the government's fight against paramilitaries or its purge of the military high command. If this is the type of peace process that is to dominate, then negotiations will be subject at best to repeated and needless interruptions and delays, and at worst to a unilateral and arbitrary evaluation of the negotiations. This runs counter to the idea of bilateral negotiation and places the government in an untenable situation vis-a-vis public opinion. In practice, the government appears to be acting defensively, while the FARC are seen as the moving force behind the talks.

There are also concerns regarding the consequences of the accords. The government talks of limited negotiations, aimed at addressing specific issues. By contrast, the FARC speak of structural reforms leading to fundamental changes within politics, society and the economy. Limited reforms aim for gradual change: their goal is to strengthen democratic institutions and encourage economic policies that will lead to greater social justice. Structural reforms, on the other hand, have no real objectives: how do we know when they have been achieved?

FARC and ELN want negotiations to take place in a context of war, while civil society demand that a bilateral ceasefire be called. For the peace process to succeed within a reasonable timeframe, it will require popular ratification, thus ensuring democratic backing, as well as a Commission of Accompaniment, a bilateral ceasefire and a delimitation of the negotiations.

The government's mistakes and the guerrillas' continued military activity, produce distrust in public opinion at home and abroad, yet the climate for peace has improved. There is a growing interest in Colombia within the EU, the US and Latin America and at the UN. This interest has led to different types of initiatives, ranging from financial aid to offers of mediation. These offers are still slim, but they are growing and, as in El Salvador and Guatemala, are likely to gain a strategic role.

Colombia is experiencing a historically unprecedented popular mobilisation against violence. On 24 October, 12 million people (30% of the population) took to the streets in protest, both in Colombia and abroad. The positive impact of mobilisations in Spain against ETA and in Peru against Shining Path has had an effect here.

The FARC and the government have agreed a negotiation agenda, and the ELN has agreed to a National Convention. In addition to these important steps, there is a willingness in the country, even among labour unions and business groups, to achieve a basic consensus. Lastly, there is a growing moderation in the rhetoric of the guerrillas and a manifest willingness to move from absolute objectives (socialism, the dictatorship of the proletariat) to relative objectives (increasing democracy and achieving social justice).

Despite this, there are a number of clouds on the horizon. The country is in the grip of the most serious economic crisis since the 1930s. Reformist policies will be difficult to implement in this context. A second concern is the threat made by Venezuela's President Hugo Chávez to give the guerrillas belligerent status, a measure of official recognition that has led to serious binational tensions and has produced heightened expectations among the armed actors. There are also fears that the recent extradition of top drug cartel bosses to the US will lead to a renewal of drug-related terrorism.

Yet the positive factors outweigh the negative and there is a sense of moderate optimism in the country. To avoid further frustration, however, the international community will have to mobilise in favour of peace. ❏

Eduardo Pizarro Leongómez *is director of the Instituto de Estudios Políticos y Relaciones Internacionales at the Universidad Nacional in Bogotá. He writes regularly on the conflict in* El Espectador. *His most recent book is* Insurgencia sin revolución *(1996). Translated by Paulo Drinot*

ALFRED MOLANO

The banishing

One million displaced Colombians are caught in the crossfire of a politics of eviction that goes back centuries. They rarely return home

The establishment chooses to view the displacement of people in Colombia as a physical phenomenon. At best, it is a geographical shift: the place of residence of the displaced changes. A closer look reveals that the very use of the term 'displaced' masks one of the most dramatic and bloody events of our times. People are not 'displaced'. They are banished, evicted, forced to flee and to hide.

It has become commonplace to view displacement as merely the outcome of the present conflict between guerrillas and paramilitaries. No mention is made of the fact that the eviction of people from their land is not a new practice. By blaming the guerrillas and the paramilitaries, responsibility is diverted from the regime, and in particular from the Colombian armed forces.

According to Eric Hobsbawm, Colombia's history is characterised by two recurring events: permanent colonisation and violence. Both the conquest and the repopulation of the colonial period support this. In the nineteenth century, these peculiarities of Colombian history became deeply ingrained. During this period, Colombia experienced 52 civil wars – and more elections than in any other country in Spanish America.

At heart conflicts between protectionists and free-traders, these wars were articulated in a political struggle between conservatism and liberalism. Control of political office, the ultimate purpose of the wars, opened the way to the accumulation of riches. In practice, the conflicts were an opportunity to expropriate the vanquished and appropriate their labour force.

The wars resulted in large movements of economic and human resources as the agricultural peons (day labourers) and sharecroppers of the vanquished were recruited by force to work in the plantations of the conqueror. Civil wars led to both depopulation and repopulation, depending on the outcome of elite political struggles. Extra-economic coercion, the use or threat of violence was instrumental in both the displacement of the peasantry and its deployment in plantations.

The violence of the 1950s was an accelerated and acute process of displacement. According to Paul Oquist, 200,000 Colombians fell victim to sectarianism and state repression, 400,000 plots of land were deserted and 2 million Colombians abandoned their land. In Valle, Tolima and Cauca lands that had belonged to peasants before the violence began came under the control of large landowners and businessmen. In the coffee-growing area, small villages and towns grew significantly. By 1964 they had become large cities. Between 1938 and 1964, Colombia experienced a rapid transition from an agrarian society to a country in an accelerated process of urbanisation. Political factors and violence appear to account for many of the demographic changes.

Today, history is repeating itself. According to a recent study by the Human Rights and Displacement Consultancy, 850,000 Colombians were displaced between 1985 and 1996; 200,000 of them in that last year alone. In the last five years, the rate of displacement has increased annually. Taking into account the average for the last few years, by the year 2000 a million people will be displaced. Significantly, the state has not carried out a census of people in this situation.

Approximately 50% of displaced persons are found in the cities of two regions characterised by a strong paramilitary presence: Urabá and Magdalena Medio. The former is a banana-growing region where fruit and food companies have made large investments. It is also a region that will host two large infrastructure projects: a road to complete the pan-American highway, linking Alaska with Tierra del Fuego, and an inter-oceanic canal that by linking the rivers Atrato and Truandó will connect the Pacific with the Atlantic. Magdalena Medio is a key land communication centre and a gas and oil production and transportation centre. It is also host to the most powerful trade union in the country. The interests of international companies, the government and the private sector converge in this region as in no other in Colombia. The displaced flee to these areas and to Bogotá. It is as if they are seeking the most remote and anonymous areas.

The role of fear in displacement is obvious. Only 8% of the displaced remain in the rural areas. Some 35% blame the paramilitaries for their expulsion, another 15% blame local police forces and 28% blame the guerrillas. It is clear that war, and in particular the military tactic of depopulation, is to blame for displacement. For 50%, threats were the cause of their leaving, another 15% blame killings. Some 45% of the displaced are 18 years or older; 33% are children younger than 10. Half of them were involved in some form of community-based organisation in their places of origin. On the Atrato River and in Magdalena Medio, both unions and the church have a long tradition and there is little doubt that these ties are targets of the paramilitaries.

Surprisingly, 40% of displaced persons have received no assistance of any kind. Most are peasants with very low incomes, with little formal education. They look for a place to live and for work, as wage earners or by setting up small businesses. The level of trust in the government is very low: only 17% are willing to return to their plots of land. Though these figures help illustrate an aspect of this drama, they are insufficient explanations of the process of displacement.

These last few years the police and armed forces have been largely responsible for the displacements. Their strategy has consisted of forcing peasants to flee in order to make their attacks on the guerrillas more effective. In many cases, the local peasantry supported the guerrillas by providing them with information and food. In turn, the guerrillas often functioned as a surrogate state, providing basic services such as health, education and conflict settlement.

Displacement usually began following the murder of local leaders. Some were disappeared, others were imprisoned and tortured. Yet another brutal and regular method used was indiscriminate aerial bombardment. In some areas the army employed tactics similar to those of the US in Vietnam: people were herded into strategic villages where their movements were tightly controlled. The outlying areas were considered no-man's-land and in many cases razed. In general, peasants were left with a single option: to flee.

And flee they did. Some to the cities where they sought housing and employment, thus increasing competition and worsening the crisis of public services. Naturally, urban crime increased in step with the newcomers' growing despair. Meanwhile, the guerrillas carried out 'cleansing' operations to expel informers and traitors. These cases grew in tandem with military intelligence and infiltration operations. A number of executions and evictions were carried out as a result. Some guerrillas used their military positions to settle personal scores. These practices have not ceased, and very little has been done to curtail them.

As 'organic' paramilitary groups have grown, the displacement of populations has become a routine military strategy. The guerrillas consider the mobilisation of the peasantry as their political goal. Mao Zedong called this relationship the fish's water. The guerrillas' enemies have caught on and reached an obvious conclusion: remove the water from the fish tank in order to asphyxiate the insurgents. The strategy is as brutal as it is simple: the most highly regarded leaders are assassinated in front of the community to set an example, houses are burnt or pillaged. Before they leave, the paramilitaries threaten to return to kill all those who aid the guerrillas. Union leaders, school teachers, doctors and nurses, priests and mayors, members of the community boards and relatives of the guerrillas have all been killed. The objective is to sever the ties between the guerrillas and the communities.

Terror brings a number of social consequences. The most important is the breakdown of solidarity and mutual co-operation based on neighbourly action, family ties, professional affinities or ideological sympathies. One of the paramilitaries' manifest objectives is to destroy all these networks. These networks, the paramilitaries understand, are the social force behind protest and resistance. When the networks are broken, distrust and recrimination set in. Community life becomes a living hell. The most obvious effect of the breakdown of community ties is the unravelling of first the extended family and then the nuclear family. Distrust and fear reach such levels that communal life becomes impossible. People feel secure only when they are alone.

The paramilitaries, who call themselves Peasant Self Defence Forces, seek to prevent any form of peasant defence. They know that the peasantry's strength lies in solidarity and it is this they seek to destroy. They justify their actions by alleging peasant collaboration with the guerrillas, with international communism or even with the drug cartels. The paramilitaries seek to eliminate protests, insubordination and rebellion, and this is why they are so warmly welcomed by the large planters, cattle raisers, merchants, foreign companies and politicians, who partly fund them.

The paramilitaries' actions are of the greatest benefit to the economic interests of the rich and powerful. The guerrillas also provide a measure of security by eliminating cattle rustlers, thieves, wrongdoers and rapists. Employers acknowledge this role. But the guerrillas do not put an end to social protests, union struggle or demands for higher wages and a better quality of life. And this is precisely what paramilitary groups do on a routine basis and to order. Paramilitaries eliminate the leaders of unconformity, they set wage levels and work contracts, prices for the peasants' products and rubber-stamp planters' interest in conflicts. A rich businessman from the banana-growing region of the country once confessed to me that the paramilitaries were better than the guerrillas because they 'obeyed' him. This is the link between the paramilitaries and the establishment. The paramilitaries represent an ever-growing sector of the establishment that has risen in arms against the National Constitution. They are not therefore a rebel group that fights the establishment – they fight the laws that restrain the establishment.

The military reacts angrily when the paramilitaries are mentioned. The military dislike the fact that the paramilitaries are called self-defence groups, because this implies that the armed forces are incapable of providing security. They prefer to call the groups 'private justice', as opposed to 'public justice' which they characterise as biased and corrupt. The principle used by the Conservative Party to justify their actions in the 1950s, the right to legitimate defence, is thus re-appropriated. In fact, those who fund the paramilitaries' operations dictate the criteria of justice that are applied. As such paramilitary justice amounts to a defence of the interests of the upper class. What is more difficult to explain is why the authorities are incapable of reducing and controlling the guerrillas.

In addition to the economic and military reasons, displacement has another cause: land usurpation. Two types prevail. The first is called *trasvase*. After the paramilitaries have cleared a region they bring peasants who are loyal to their cause and allow them to take over the land and other possessions left behind by the evicted peasants. The paramilitaries thus gain loyal supporters; sometimes they even implement token agrarian reforms. In the second, it is landlords who finance the paramilitaries' campaigns who usurp the peasantry's land. This is the most common type of usurpation, particularly when the lands are valuable or strategically situated, or when a major infrastructure work is envisaged that will add value to the land. Yet another case of displacement takes place around the construction of large hydroelectric or road-building projects, where lands are cleared to avoid protests, complaints and riots while at the same time ensuring the smooth operation of the works.

There is a clear link between the drug trade and displacement. Drug bosses are the legitimate owners of some five million hectares of highly prized land, a by-product of their criminal activities. Arguably, these lands are the money box of drug trafficking. Given that the authorities are obliged to indict these criminals and that the guerrilla is a sworn enemy of large landowners, drug bosses have little choice but to defend themselves by resorting to paramilitary groups. They can count on impunity, or more to the point, on the army's institutional tolerance, which guarantees that their interests are protected. The paramilitaries are a channel through which the drug cartels corrupt public authorities

and, to some extent, make them work for them. In this way, the strengthening of the paramilitaries is a direct cause of the cruel and escalating large-scale eviction of people from the countryside.

The absence of a policy that envisages a curb on paramilitary activity amounts to the most embarrassing form of impunity. By formulating remedial programmes to deal with displacement, rather than addressing its root causes, the government is effectively legitimising it. Rather than trying to reverse and control the process of displacement, the Colombian

Returnees examine a deserted riverside village of Punte America –
Credit: Phillip Jones Griffiths/Magnum

state has opted for assistance programmes that will do little to help the displaced. ❏

Alfredo Molano *is a columnist with* El Espectador *and author of a number of oral histories of Colombia's recent violence. Translated by Paulo Drinot*

ANONYMOUS

In the battalion

A Colombian journalist meets a disaffected soldier in oil-rich Barrancabermeja, a city long targeted by the paramilitaries as a forcing ground for members of the rebel National Liberation Army (ELN). He tells how the US-backed army and the murderous paramilitaries work together like the fingers of the same bloody fist

WHAT ARE YOUR MEMORIES OF YOUR FIRST DAYS IN THE ARMY?

As soon as we arrived we were sent to a training camp. We were trained in counter-guerrilla tactics and did combat training with blanks. They told us that anyone involved in human rights was a guerrilla. Anyone who was a peasant was also a guerrilla as far as we were concerned. They trained us to kill. Whenever you went into operations you took a *rifle de cuadre*.

WHAT'S THAT?

You took an extra rifle. If there were operations but no action, you killed a peasant and you gave them the rifle and dressed them in camouflage. Whenever there was a military target and you didn't kill anyone, you had to take back a body. That's how we did it.

WHO DID YOU KILL?

Whoever. When there was fighting we were there in support and, when it was all over, we would stay in the mountains as infiltrators or ambushers. The last time we killed an old man, a hunchback. We were after a commander of the *Elenos* (ELN). We couldn't find him so we grabbed an old man instead because he had the same surname on his ID card. My lieutenant told me to kill him, if I had the guts. I said: 'If I have to, I have to.' But he gave the order to another soldier.

AND THEN REPORTED THAT HE HAD BEEN KILLED IN COMBAT?

Of course. You set up simulated crossfire in case there is an investigation. You set off an alarm, four or five shots from each soldier. It's a sham but the lieutenant gets promotion.

PROMOTION DEPENDS ON THE NUMBER OF BODIES YOU BRING BACK?

Yes. My first experience of the way things worked was when we were in a joint operation with the Tayrona battalion, which I think is from the Magdalena. There had been fighting in the Sierra Nevada, fierce, bloody combat with the guerrillas. The battalion had blocked the guerrilla's supply routes, working with the *paracos* [paramilitaries]. The guerrillas were starting to die. They were really hungry and worn down. We went up when the fighting was over, then retreated and the *paracos* went in with the battalion. They massacred the peasants. About 15 of them.

HOW DO THE PARACOS FUNCTION?

The *paracos* in the battalion buy the arms.

THE ARMY KNOWS WHO THEY ARE?

Of course. They go on manoeuvres with the battalion. They borrow the battalion's cars to travel to other regions.

IS THERE A PARAMILITARY BASE THERE?

Lucas Gnneco the governor [of Cesar] has his base there. He pays for the *paracos*, he finances them.

AND HOW DO YOU KNOW THIS?

I got friendly with a first lieutenant who had a lot of information. Gnneco was involved in the death of a human rights journalist who had information that he was financing the paramilitaries in Valledupar. One day I overheard two colonels in the battalion talking about it.

Two *paracos* arrived and took a couple of pistols that had belonged to the guerrilla we'd captured. They needed guns that couldn't be traced because there was an investigation going on. They stayed in the battalion for seven days training us. We were always chatting with them, asking them what they had done. They offered us money and said that as soon as we left the military we could join them.

HOW ARE THE PARACOS ORGANISED IN THAT AREA?

By *barrio*. Everything in Cesar is run by Gnneco. He finances and gets the uniforms for the battalion, and he distributes stuff to the other paramilitaries.

HOW MUCH DOES A PARACO EARN?

At the start they earn about 340,000 pesos (around US$190). A really fearless killer will get promoted to leader and his wages will go up. Whenever the *paracos* get a tip off, they travel together in the battalion's transport, the army on one side, them on the other.

The *paraco* I was talking to asked why I didn't work with them. He knew that I was from the local *barrios* [the *communa*s of Barrancabermeja] and that I would know where the guerrilla commanders lived, where the collaborators lived. He said: 'Why don't you earn some good money, you idiot. Go and join the *paracos* in Nueva Granada.'

AND HOW DOES THEIR TRAINING CONTINUE? DO THEY TELL THEM THAT THEY ARE PARACOS?

I don't know where they do their training, the information is closely guarded. They always take reservists because then they are already trained. And those that go who haven't done military service, they get intensively trained. As soon as you get there they say that the first thing you have to do is kill someone in cold blood. It brainwashes you. It was the *paracos* who taught us how to torture people.

WHAT DID THEY TELL YOU?

To torture someone you tie them up and you give them electric shocks on the tongue to make them talk. When they refuse to talk, you use those big long needles [he indicates the size of his index finger], and stab the needles through their nails. Then you strip them and make them sit on a block of ice. And when they still won't give you information then you castrate them and pour acid over them so that they end up completely disfigured, so that no one is implicated. The *paracos* have always done it. Recently in the Cesar, near Media Luna, they burned a whole family with acid. I was in the battalion there and a soldier told me about it. He said the son was a guerrilla and that the *paracos* were furious with him because he had killed one of their commanders. So they went into the house and dragged out the whole family. There were three young kids and they threw acid on all of them. Acid like that turns a person black.

WHO ARE THE INFORMERS?

They are always volunteers. If you have a good tip-off you go to the battalion and they give you camouflage and let you direct the operation. If it comes off, then you get paid. The first time the *paracos* pay you up to 700,000 pesos (US$395). But after two months they reduce the money to about 300,000. Then you can't leave, because you're implicated.

WHAT DID YOU HEAR ABOUT PLACES LIKE BARRANCA?

'Man, it would be great if Ecopetrol blew up so that those sons of bitches burn,' as they'd say. For them, everyone from Barranca is a guerrilla.

HOW DO THEY TALK ABOUT PEASANTS? HOW DO THEY DESCRIBE THEM?

Union members, guerrillas, the USO [oil workers union] they are all the same for the *paracos*. They're seen as collaborators and military targets.

ARE THERE A LOT OF RETIRED MILITARY PERSONNEL IN THE PARACOS?

Phew, almost all of the leaders in the *paracos* are retired lieutenants or sergeants, officers. That's why they are so well trained. It's a real advantage to have someone who knows about combat and patrols.

WHAT DO YOU KNOW ABOUT A MASSACRE BEING PLANNED FOR BARRANCA?

There are soldiers who have joined, volunteers, they're planning to return to Barranca, to infiltrate the area. They'll work with the guerrillas for a bit and get to know what's going on so that they can hit them hard. But it will be the *paracos* who do that, they won't involve the army.

AND IS THERE MUCH INFILTRATION?

Yes, whoever wants to can join the guerrillas and it's a disaster. The *paracos'* objective is guerrilla collaborators. But it's not the collaborators they'll kill, it's the ordinary people at home.

DO THE OFFICERS THINK THEY ARE LOSING OR WINNING THE WAR?

As an army they're lost. They themselves say so, my major said to us, here I am, I'm going to be handing over to Mono Jojoy [ELN leader]. They realise that the guerrillas are really on the up and they are effectively losing the war. There's been a lot of setbacks. Your average military man is only interested in earning a wage, nothing else. They don't feel like they used to, that they were the army, that they loved their country.

WHEN DO YOU THINK THE MASSACRES ARE GOING TO HAPPEN, THE ONES THEY'RE PLANNING?

They're planned for the end of December. But we're talking about a huge massacre, one that will be felt all over the country. The one that they're going to commit in Barranca, adding it all up, is going to hit around 100 people – they're going to go into all the *barrios*.

ARE THE PEOPLE PREPARED? DO THEY KNOW?
No, they know nothing, I'm the only one with the information. If I were to tell anyone the *paracos* would soon send someone for me.

WHAT'S LIFE LIKE IN THE MOUNTAINS? DO YOU GET HUNGRY, IS IT HARD WORK?
Yes. The officers steal the money for fresh food. Always rice, potatoes, sardines, that was the food every day. Sometimes there was only rice because there was no money to buy things.

WHAT IS LIFE LIKE FOR YOUNG PEOPLE IN THE BARRIOS?
For young people here it's all about being in the guerrillas, carrying a gun, intimidating civilians. They want to feel good. But when they have to fight they can't. They look down on me because I've just left. I won't do anyone any favours, won't hang around with them. Why would I want to get involved in that stuff? If I decide to join the guerrillas I'll take my gun and go to the mountains. But not here, because here they only kill innocent people.

WHAT SORT OF AGE ARE MOST OF THE PARACOS?
Mostly young – mainly reservists. The leaders are older. They're bloodthirsty. The counter-guerrilla paramilitaries carry chainsaws with them, about this size [he indicates his forearm], for cutting people up. Any *paraco* that goes on operations takes one with him. They have mass graves, over in the Centre [Barranca].

DO THEY USE ANY AS INFORMERS?
Sure, there were several in that group who changed sides, the *paracos* were going to kill them so they changed sides. But they don't take just anyone as an informer. Mostly it's the peasants who are infiltrators. Because anyone who gives a good tip off gets well paid, when it pays off. Really really good information, with casualties, that's worth around 1 million pesos (US$560). So it's really tempting. ❏

The anonymous interviewer is a reputable Colombian war journalist. Index on Censorship *checked his bona fides, possesses a tape of the interview and has submitted this edited text to Amnesty International, Human Rights Watch and Christian Aid for confirmation of authenticity. To publish such information in a Colombian newspaper is to court execution: 50 Colombian journalists have been murdered during the past 10 years. Translated by Madeleine Church*

RICHARD SANDERS

The emerald lords

Colombia's emerald zone is a bizarre, medieval world, marooned in the mountains and ruled by the gun

A miner emerges from the mouth of a tunnel, bent double beneath a sack of earth. He staggers to the ravine and cracks open the sack, spilling dirt down to a stream at the bottom. Instantly, the dirt is submerged beneath a swarm of thin figures, scrabbling at the earth with their fingers.

This is Coscuez Emerald Mine and word has spread that a fresh seam has been struck. Scavengers have gathered from miles around. The waste thrown from the mine entrance is suddenly gold dust and, if they can find just a few emerald chips, it could mean the difference between eating and starving.

Less than a mile away, on a hill above the mine, sits the plump figure of Don Pablo Elias Delgadillo, the owner of Coscuez. Guards lounge nonchalantly nearby. A young blonde sits at his side, filing her nails. 'Inside the mine there is great wealth,' sighs Don Pablo philosophically, 'but outside there is great poverty.'

Nestling in the lower Andes, 100 miles north of Bogotá, this is the world's foremost emerald region, accounting for two-thirds of global production. A trip to the emerald face at Coscuez, which produces half of the region's jewels, is a battle against claustrophobia and vertigo. Water rushes round your feet as you slither along miles of narrow tunnels. Greasy, 35-metre-long ladders plunge down into the darkness. At the end of the last tunnel stands Pedro, gasping in foetid air as he drills at the rock.

'The truth is that we don't get a salary,' he says. 'If emeralds appear, we get a bonus, we get a part of the emeralds. And we grab what we can from the floor. But if there is no production, well, it's tough.' That day, the white emerald-bearing seams showed, but the emeralds were elusive.

It's a no-lose situation for the owners but for the scavengers outside – the *guaqueros* – even this seems a privilege. Stories abound of families who have handed a daughter to the mine owner in return for a job underground. Access is everything. At night the *guaqueros* seek out hidden shafts, some dug hundreds of years ago by the Indians, and break through into the main tunnels.

Ruben works as a mine guard. 'Last week one of my mates was on duty when he heard a sound in one of the tunnels. He rushed down and someone stuck a gun in the back of his neck. "Please, I have a wife and children," he said. So they let him go. He was lucky.' Often at night the mine shafts ring to the sound of gunshots. Sometimes there are fights. 'A couple of miners might stumble across a big emerald,' Ruben continues. 'They agree to split it but then, as they are walking back to the surface, one is killed in a mysterious rock fall. The other is left unscathed.' He shrugs.

This is the wild frontier of the most violent country on earth and almost everyone is armed. Many are on the run from the law and only the awesome power of the mine owners – or *patróns* – keeps the peace. 'It's like this,' Ruben's mate Jaime explains. 'Each *patrón* has his own group of people and you have to answer to your *patrón* for what you do. Strangers are killed, no questions asked,' he says.

I stumbled across a corpse at dawn in the morning drizzle. The man had been killed in a gunfight a few hours before. His drinking partner had dressed him in his best clothes and laid him out on a couple of beer crates for an impromptu wake. As I turned to leave, I was surrounded by armed men demanding to know why I was there. I explained that I was a guest of Don Pablo's but one of the gunmen cut me off. He said 'Don Pablo is the boss on the hill. Down here you answer to Don Martin,' jerking his thumb at a figure with a poncho and a moustache. I had crossed the invisible line between emerald fiefdoms. I was allowed to leave only when I had convinced Don Martin I wasn't investigating the killing. 'That's my business,' he said.

In its strict hierarchy and code of honour the emerald business mirrors the hidden world of the drug cartels and a number of *patróns* are suspected of narcotics links. They are also believed to be among the most powerful paramilitary warlords, mustering private armies to combat the guerrilla movements. At the pinnacle sits Victor Carranza, estimated by

Forbes magazine to be one of the richest men in the world. Like most *patróns*, Carranza is of humble origin and his life story is an inspiration for every *guaquero*. It was said that, if he stood in the Plaza Bolivar in Bogotá long enough, emeralds would appear. By the 1980s, he'd clawed his way to the top of the emerald ladder. When drug traffickers from Medellin tried to muscle in 10 years ago, Carranza led the resistance. Around 5,000 people died in what was only the most recent in a series of emerald wars. The victims included miners, *guaqueros*, bodyguards and paramilitaries.

Today Carranza is in jail, accused of organising paramilitary groups. Don Pablo represents his interests in emerald country and so is now de facto 'don of dons'. But he knows better than to usurp the authority of his boss. 'Although he's in jail Don Victor is irreplaceable. He is a man of wisdom, a man we go to for advice,' he says. 'He is like a father to us.'

'Don Victor's problems are political rather than judicial,' he tells me. 'There's been a lot of international pressure, especially from NGOs, about human rights.' He's confident that Don Victor will be released soon and he's probably right. The public prosecutor's office is making desperate efforts to keep the identity of the sole witness against Carranza a secret, but few would lay odds on his surviving to give testimony.

Don Pablo presents his own power as a burden. 'I run the company but I also have to attend to 90% of the social, economic, family and moral problems that arise. I am mayor, judge, everything.' Watching the *guaqueros* knee-deep in the water, sifting through the mud from the mine entrance, it's impossible to tell if these emotions are reciprocated, such is the people's poverty. All live in hope of one chance discovery that will transform their lives.

'That's the life of the mine,' shrugs Pedro, as he raises his drill once more to the emerald face. 'No one makes you work here.' ❑

Richard Sanders is a journalist and television producer. He worked in Colombia in 1995 and 1996 and presented the Channel 4 documentary Escobar's Own Goal, *about the murder of footballer Andres Escobar*

SIMEON TEGEL

Ley of the land

A film attacking Mexico's governing party is under attack from its co-producers, who dislike its revised ending – now why could that be?

As an attack on the party which has ruled Mexico for more than 70 years, *La Ley de Herodes* could not be more direct. For the first time in the country's history, a film-maker has dared to use the name of the Partido Revolucionario Institucional (Institutional Revolutionary Party) or PRI in a fierce political satire.

Set in the 1940s, *La Ley* follows Juan Vargas, the mediocre *Priista* mayor of the village of San Pedro de los Saguaros, as he naively struggles to bring 'modernisation and social justice' to the rural backwater. Despite his best intentions, Vargas gradually becomes corrupted by the system. By the end he is taking bribes, framing opponents, sleeping with prostitutes and flinging racist curses at the local Indians, all the while ranting about the 'hypocrisy' of his political adversaries.

There is no doubt that the PRI is *La Ley's* main target. Armed with a pistol and a copy of the Mexican constitution, Vargas wears a party pin in his lapel and at one stage drops it incriminatingly at the scene of a double murder. No wonder the film, which was struggling to find a distributor, is at the centre of a fierce censorship row.

The first and only public showing of *La Ley* – the title, Herod's Law, refers to a crude Mexican saying which could be translated as 'Either you're screwed or you're buggered' – was during a festival of French and domestic films in Acapulco on 12 November. It played to an enraptured and overflowing house of more than 1,000 viewers, but the screening nearly didn't take place.

Just 24 hours earlier state-funded co-producers Imcine announced that the work was being dropped from the festival because of 'technical problems'. Word of the film's strong political content had already leaked out and soon the 'censorship' of *La Ley* was the talking point of the festival. The next morning, following press criticism and strong support from European delegates, including the Spanish actress Victoria Abril, the film was reinstated. A general release date, however, looks increasingly distant.

Whether Imcine simply got cold feet or whether there was pressure from above remains a mystery, but the bungled bid to drop the film led director Luis Estrada and actor Damián Alcázar to joke darkly that the row had been a marketing ploy. The official reason for Imcine's displeasure is that the film's ending, which sees Vargas rewarded with a seat in the congress, was different from that originally approved by Imcine (in which he winds up in jail). But the director insists that he kept Imcine informed of any changes to the script as it was being made.

La Ley takes swipes at plenty of targets. The village doctor, a member of the Republican-inspired National Action Party (PAN), is a paedophile while the local priest is seen swapping benedictions for cash. Meanwhile, in a possible attack on the PRI's leading left-of-centre opponent, Cuauhtémoc Cárdenas, a *Priista* governor defects to set up his own party when his presidential ambition is thwarted.

Nevertheless, what makes *La Ley* unique in Mexican cinema is the explicit nature of its assault on the PRI. The country's most celebrated political drama, *La Sombra del Caudillo*, was banned for 30 years despite being regarded by some commentators as more historical than topical. Made in 1960 by director Julio Bracho, it dealt with a general's power struggle in the 1920s, just before the birth of the party that was to become the PRI. Clearly based on events at the end of the presidency of General Alvaro Obregón in 1924, the film changed the protagonists' names. But it was banned, apparently at the behest of the Mexican army, until October 1990 when an inexplicably poor quality copy was screened publicly for the first time.

More recently, Jorge Fons's 1989 *Rojo Amanecer*, a gritty drama based around the 1968 Tlatelolco massacre, challenged the establishment, though in a less direct way than *La Ley*. The film follows a family living in Mexico City's Tlatelolco square through the events of 2 October 1968, when an estimated 300 anti-government protestors were killed just months before Mexico hosted the Olympics. The atrocity traumatised Mexico more than any other event since the revolution, with the possible exception of the 1985 earthquake, and to this day remains the single biggest blow to the PRI's legitimacy. But, judging by the cuts imposed on *Rojo Amanecer*, the movie was officially viewed as a greater threat to the military establishment than to the political one.

'*La Ley* is a milestone,' said Leonardo García Tsao, *Variety's* Mexican film reviewer. 'We will have to see what happens but this could be the beginning of something. Other film-makers may now see this film and think,"Yes, I can get away with that."'

Carlos Bonfil, film critic of the leading Mexican daily, *La Jornada*, agrees. 'This is definitely a watershed. Five years ago a film like this would not have been made. A screenwriter would simply have known that he would not get a distributor ... And there is no way that Imcine would have been involved either.'

La Ley comes at a time of democratic reform in Mexico, with the PRI's presidential candidate, Francisco Labastida, chosen by the party's first nationwide primary rather than the traditional *dedazo* ('big finger') by which the outgoing president personally picked his successor. But old habits die hard. Just one week before the row over *La Ley* exploded, several radio and television stations dropped a hard-hitting political ad from PAN. The ad, which quoted the campaign promises of the last five presidents, using their own words against them, was eventually shown but only after PAN accused interior minister Jorge Alcocer of interference.

La Ley de Herodes – Credit: Hildegard Oloarte

According to Estrada *La Ley* has already been invited to next year's Sundance festival in the US and now the battle is on to secure a general release for the film in Mexico. Distributors, including Hollywood's Fox and Columbia which have a big presence in Mexico, are interested in the film. However, that interest is being kept quiet while the row over the final version continues with Imcine.

Estrada has fiercely resisted proposed changes, some of which are highly impractical (such as relocating the film to a country other than Mexico). 'All I want to do is protect this film. I made it the way it is for certain reasons and I don't want to change it,' he said.

'The response to the film has been like Dr Jekyll and Mr Hyde. The critics, the public and the distributors have all liked it. But then I am having to deal with Imcine.

'It is not just Imcine. It is the whole system. I knew this was a film which some people would not like and which would make people uncomfortable but I never expected this. The intolerance and lack of common sense is incredible. The question behind all this is simple: are we going to become a real democracy or will we stay in the prehistory of authoritarianism?' ❏

Simeon Tegel is Variety's *Mexico correspondent and a freelance writer*

GARETH SMYTH

Yusef in the dock

'My city does not contain me, nor my country,' claims Marcel Khalife, but his song still landed him in a Beirut court

The trial of singer Marcel Khalife on a charge of slandering Islam is the latest example of Lebanon's sectarian political system bending to pressure from religious leaders to curtail free expression. It comes as a further blow to the country's reputation as a relative haven of freedom of speech in the Arab world.

Khalife is well known for songs that express in simple human terms the nationalist sentiments of the 1970s and 1980s. At 49, he retains his ability to move people and create the lithe phrasing that took 'Ummi' (My Mother), 'Rita' and other songs into every home, café and service taxi. But Khalife's long-standing secularism sits uneasily in a society where religious affiliation permeates every aspect of life.

The song that landed Khalife in court, 'Oh My Father, I am Yusef', is based on a poem by the Palestinian Mahmoud Darwish about the persecution of Yusef, or Joseph, a well-known figure from the Old Testament and then the Quran. The poem quotes directly from the Quran, and some authorities forbid putting the Quran to music.

The complaint was filed originally in 1996 when Khalife released the song on his album *Rakwet Arab* (Arabic Coffee Pot). Legal proceedings were dropped, reportedly after pressure from the then prime minister, Rafik Hariri. But, in a surprise move, Beirut's chief investigating magistrate, Abdel Rahman Chehab, renewed the charge in October, apparently after a complaint by the Grand Mufti Sheikh Mohammed Rashid Qabbani, head of Dar el Fatwa, Lebanon's leading body of Sunni Islam.

Some Muslim leaders publicly disagree with the prosecution. Shiite cleric Sayyed Mohammed Hussein Fadlallah denied that Khalife had insulted Islam: 'Performing a poem, including a verse from the Holy Quran, is not an offence when it deals with humanitarian concerns.' Another Shiite cleric, Sheikh Mohammed Mehdi Shamseddine, agreed with Dar el Fatwa's ruling, but said that the case should not be taken to the civil courts. Leftist MP Najah Wakim was less impressed. 'I respect religious leaders but they are no closer to God than anyone else. Didn't some of them form militias and sanction sectarian cleansing during the war?' Wakim's approach is unusual. Defenders of Khalife have tended to stress his support for the Palestinians; few have challenged the right of religious leaders to threaten freedom of speech.

The Lebanese state is based on a system of 'confessionalism' by which every citizen must be a member of one of 18 religious groups. Parliamentary seats, cabinet positions and civil service jobs are allocated on religious affiliation. Personal and family law are in the hands of religious courts, and there is no civil marriage.

Khalife does not easily fit such a system – either as musician or political figure. He was born a Maronite Christian in the village of Amchit north of Beirut. In the 1970s, in opposition to most Christians, he chose the 'Arab nationalist' side, along with the Palestinians and Muslims. When war erupted in 1975, Khalife had to cross the 'green line' to live in the Muslim west.

In those days, 'nationalists' believed that confessionalism should go. But the system survived the 1975–90 civil war and is now accepted by the politicians, who are among its main beneficiaries. In the past year, Christian and Muslim religious leaders have combined to block proposals for the introduction of civil marriage. Khalife has stuck to his principles as a secularist who rejects such divisions.

The initial hearing in early November postponed the trial to 1 December to give Khalife's lawyers time to prepare their defence, and there have been rumours that Khalife would agree not to perform the song in public in return for the dropping of the charges against him.

When I met Khalife recently, he stressed that he would not give up his right to sing the song. 'I have no aim of offending any religion,' he said. 'I am a secular person and I respect and understand others. I work with the poetry of Mahmoud Darwish because it speaks about the human being in every time and place. These are not poems with a specific meaning.' This surely hints at what is at stake in the trial.

'My work represents a human work larger than the Arab world,'

Marcel Khalife – Credit: Gareth Smythe

Khalife continued. 'My city does not contain me, nor my country. I don't like borders, I don't like divisions. I communicate as a human being. I feel that this trial is a kind of international marginalisation of people – pushing people back within borders.'

Khalife's sentiments are in contrast to a ruling class that uses 'nationalism', flags and speeches to coat a politics based on sectarian calculations. Khalife is no tub-thumper. The words of 'Oh My Father, I am Yusef' refer implicitly to the oppression of the Palestinians by the Israelis (the 'wolf'), but they also appear to condemn the Palestinians' fellow Arabs for abandoning their cause.

'People talk a lot these days about nationalist songs,' Khalife said at the Deir al-Qamar festival in Lebanon this summer. 'Well, I will sing nationalist songs.' And he sang 'The Child and the Plane' in which a child confuses a kite with a swooping instrument of war.

If found guilty, Khalife could face up to three years in prison. 'The real shame,' he said, 'is that this has gone to court at all. This is an ethical

Oh My Father, I am Yusef

When the breeze passed through my hair
  They were jealous and rebelled against me
My father, I am Yusef, my father
My brothers don't love me, my father,
Oh my father.

They attack me, they throw stones at me,
They want to kill me. They have locked your door,
And I'm outside.
They have expelled me from the field,
They have given my grapes away.
They don't love me and don't want me to be among them.
Oh father.

The butterflies lay on my shoulders and the birds
Floated around me, and they greeted me.
So what have I done, my father, my father?
You have named me Yusef, father.
They have made me fall down and have accused the wolf,
But the wolf is more merciful than them, my father.

Did I commit a crime against anyone
When I said that I have seen 11 stars and the sun and moon
Kneeling for me?
I have seen 11 stars and the sun and moon,
I have seen them kneeling for me.
I have seen 11 stars and the sun and moon,
I have seen them kneeling for me. ❏

*'Oh My Father, I am Yusef', is based on a poem by **Mahmoud Darwish**, published in 1996 in the collection* Ward Aqal (Fewer Flowers)*. It is set to music by **Marcel Khalife**. The quotation from the Quran appears at the end of the poem: 'I have seen 11 stars and the sun and moon/I have seen them kneeling for me' (Yusef sura, verse 3). Translated by Zeinab Charafeddine*

and cultural scandal for Lebanon first, and then for the whole Arab world. There is in the Arab countries a censor who directs his scissors towards poems, films, the novel – and that's a real problem. Let us liberate creation.'

The Khalife trial reflects a trend towards greater censorship resulting from the often chaotic pressure of sectarian groups, rather than any concerted plan by the authorities. The Sunnites feel they have been losing out politically in the past year, and Mufti Qabbani may have a very parochial reason vis-a-vis other groups or within the Sunnite community itself for raising the issue.

Censorship is a fairly arbitrary process. There is clear, often obsessive, censorship of matters dealing with Israel, to the point of banning a Greenpeace film about the Israelis dumping waste in the Mediterranean. But all else lies in the hands of medium-level officials at General Security, who work with ill-defined guidelines. In October, the General Security cut *Civilised People*, a film directed by Randa Sabbag and set in the civil war, from 90 to 43 minutes because of bad language and 'inflammatory remarks' against Christ, the Virgin Mary and Islam. Sabbag claimed the General Security had told her: 'It's not a correct movie about the war. There's no hero.'

Also in October exhibits in an art show on the seafront corniche were withdrawn after complaints from a local mosque. Ceramic tiles proclaiming 'We are the embodiment of infinity' in an installation by Nelly Chemaly were taken as 'denying God', and Tony Chakar's golden statue of a Roman goddess was considered offensive because human representations are forbidden under Islam.

Such cases are less publicised than that of Marcel Khalife but no artist or musician doubts the importance of his trial. Khalife is famous and associated with popular Arab causes. If he can be broken, less well-known and less popular figures will think long and hard before they express themselves artistically. ❏

● *On 15 December the court found Marcel Khalife innocent of offending Islam. 'The accused sang solemnly the holy Quranic verses, therefore he did not insult the sanctity of the Quran,' the judge said*

Gareth Smyth *is the Beirut correspondent of* Arabies Trends *magazine and a regular contributor to BBC radio.*

BARRY LOWE

The area

**Santa Teresita hides its secret behind guarded iron doors. A
densely packed slum district in the northern Philippine city of
Angeles, locals know the place as the Area. Behind its fortress-
like exterior are hundreds of women and girls, kept against their
will as sex slaves in one of the biggest and most highly
organised slavery operations in the world. Unconnected with the
prostitution that is centred on the bar and disco district of
Fields Avenue, the Area caters secretly and exclusively to local
patrons, who are carefully screened before they can enter**

**Alejandro is a local businessman, operating a bakery in Angeles
City:**

> I send my men to the Area as a way of paying them a bonus. I pay
> for them to have a good time in there. It's my way of thanking
> them for their good work. They appreciate it. It's good for morale
> in the bakery.

**Susan Pineda is the founder and executive director of the
Angeles women's rights foundation, Ing Makababaying Aksyon
(Action for Women) – IMA:**

> There are about 500 women and girls inside. One reporter who
> went in pretending to be a customer was told there was even a
> six-year-old girl for sale, for just 100 pesos (US$2.50). There are
> many more between the ages of 10 and 15. Most of the women
> and girls are what we call *pronbies* or provincials: naive, poorly
> educated girls from the more backward provinces.
>
> They are made to service the Area's clients in tiny rooms with
> just enough room to lay a mattress on the floor. These are called
> *bartalinas* – pigpens. They can't get out. The few exit points are

constantly guarded.

Generally the women don't get paid. But after they've been inside for a few years and seem prepared to accept their fate they may be given small amounts of money, about 30 pesos from each client fee. They're given drugs like *shabu* (crystal amphetamine) to ease the pain. They soon become addicted.

Josie is a 17-year-old former sex slave. A few months ago she was freed in a police raid prompted by a TV report on the Area. She is being sheltered by IMA:

I come from Zamboanga, in the far south of the Philippines. My father is a farmer. I only completed elementary school. I ran away from home because of the constant quarrels between my parents and my step-brothers … I went to my aunt in General Santos City and she suggested I go to Manila where I could find work in a factory. I went to Manila and found a job but lost it soon afterwards. I met another girl from Zamboanga and we used to go together to Luneta (a large public park). One day two men, called Eugene and Rey, approached us and offered to buy us snacks. Eugene called a taxi … He said if we got in he would take us to a place where we would get jobs with high salaries. Because we badly needed jobs we decided not to ask any questions.

The car took us to Angeles. I was taken into a room and introduced to a woman called Myrna who said she was the manager. She told me my job was easy, all I had to do was eat and sleep. Myrna took me to a small room then she brought a man in and told me I had to have sex with him. I couldn't leave, I had no choice …

One day a customer came in and told me he was a TV reporter from *Inside Story*. He told me if I gave him information he would help get me out. I helped him and later the police came in and freed me together with four other girls.

Nora, 21, from Antipolo near Manila, is another former Area sex slave now in IMA's care. She left school after Grade Three and worked as a household helper in a succession of jobs that eventually brought her to Angeles:

One day a man approached me in the street and said he wanted to talk to me. His name was Rey Onday and he took me to Astro Park where he told me he could get me a job … He took me to a house in Santa Teresita … took me into one of the rooms and began to assault me … He did it many times over the next few days and told me if I disobeyed him something bad would happen to me. The he started to bring other men into the room and told me I had to give them sex. The men paid 100 pesos (US$2.50) but I didn't get the money.

Carlo is one of the Area's pimps:
We look after them and find the customers for them. Then after sex we give them a few pesos to buy some noodles. That's enough for them. They don't complain.

Norma, 51, once worked as a prostitute. Today she runs a fast food outlet in Fields Avenue. Many of her customers are sex workers. She came to Angeles 17 years ago:
I tried to leave a few times but then I realised I would never leave. Now it's ok. I have my own life here. It's enough for me to support my children. I first came here when my husband left me for another woman. I had two children and I was desperate … It started for me on 16 December 1982 – I still remember that day – the day I had my first client. It was close to Christmas and I needed money for food for my children. I had no other choice.

Marites, 20, comes from Northern Samar, one of the Philippines' poorest provinces. She spent two months in the Area before being freed by police:
I had a number of jobs working in Manila as a household helper. I quit my last job because the work was too hard … I went to stay with my sister but her husband didn't want me there and we had a quarrel. So I went to sleep the night at Luneta Park. I met a man there who said he could get me a job as a waitress in Angeles City. He took me to a house in Angeles and introduced me to the manager Myrna. Myrna put me into a very small room where I had to entertain men. It went on night and day, if you liked it or not. I wanted to escape but the house was always guarded. I was a prisoner.

Sonny Lopez is a local political figure and a former Angeles City councillor:

You should understand that this is our tradition here. We believe that the young men should go to the Area to be 'baptised'. This is the tradition – it's been like that for a long time.

Moning, 20, the daughter of a farmer from Davao del Sur in the southern Philippines, was also contacted by one of the Area's recruiters in Luneta Park:

Right away I understood that the place he brought me to was a house of prostitution and I tried to resist. But they threatened to harm me if I didn't do what they wanted. I was taken into a room and forced to have sex with some customers. I wanted to escape but there were always people watching me. I knew that if I tried to get out they would stop me and take me back. Even if I did get out where would I go? I didn't know the place at all. One of my clients felt sorry for me and asked Myrna if she would let me go and allow me to start a new life. But Myrna said I couldn't go unless I paid her back the money I owed her for food and lodging. I became pregnant but I still had to entertain clients, even though it was very painful for me.

Norma:

I started to work from one of the bars, meeting men and going out with them. One day an Australian took me out … He wanted to keep me with him; he wouldn't let me go back to the bar. But after a month he went back to Australia which meant I had to go back to the bar. But he left me with an Australian souvenir. She's 12 years old now and her name is Deborah.

Another Australian I met decided to stay in Angeles and he bought his own bar, appointing me as manager. But after a while he also left and the bar closed down and I had to go back to my old work again. I stopped 'working' in 1994. Since then, I've been a hotel chambermaid, a waitress and now a fast food cook.

Susan Pineda:

There are about 200 *casas* – flimsy structures of plywood and roofing iron – inside the Area and the whole Santa Teresita community is dependent on the income they get from selling the women. It is a community of pimps and mama-sans.

Tina, 31, from the sugar-growing province of Negros Occidental, is the oldest of the five escapees:

I was working in a 24-hour canteen that catered for taxi drivers in Caloocan (in northern Manila) while living in Cavite (south of Manila). It was a long way for me to commute, particularly when I had to work night shifts. One night I was waiting for a jeepney (public minibus)] near Luneta when a man approached me and started talking to me ... Then my jeepney came and he insisted on boarding with me. He asked me to go to a restaurant with him but I refused. He followed me when I got into my second jeepney. He kept insisting I go with him. Then he said he would find my children and harm them if I didn't do what he said. So I agreed to go with him to a restaurant. But the taxi took us to an isolated grassy spot where he sexually assaulted me. He said he was going to take me somewhere where I would have a high paying job. We got to Angeles early in the morning. I was forced to work as a prostitute. I often thought about escaping but the pimps were always watching me.

Susan Pineda:

The Area is run by a group of former police officers. The big boss is a former colonel. The syndicate has close links with the city's police force and pays for police protection. Which is why nothing ever gets done to close the place down.'
❏

Barry Lowe is a lecturer in journalism at the City University of Hong Kong

PAUL BOWLES

Lines of flight

Paul and Jane Bowles moved from New York to Tangiers in 1947, attracted both by expatriate life in postwar Morocco and a society unusually tolerant of homosexuality. Though most famous for *The Sheltering Sky*, his first novel published in 1949, Paul Bowles began as a composer of songs, concertos and incidental theatre music before switching to writing. Over the next half-century, he wrote five novels and 10 collections of short stories, while translating the stories of Moroccan writers such as Mohammed Mrabet. Paul Bowles died of a heart attack in Tangiers hospital on 18 November 1999.

Paul Bowles signing prints of his photographs, Tangier, 1990 – Credit: Simon Bischoff

'Probably the most intensely poetic spot I had ever seen.' Taghit, Algeria, 1947 – Credit: Paul Bowles

Jane Bowles (left) and Cherifa in the street, Tangier, 1957 – Credit: Terence Spencer

'On 4th April 1957, she suffered a stroke. The circumstances were mysterious; there were rumours that she had been poisoned by Cherifa. Such incidents were not uncommon in Morocco, where women practiced magic.' *Simon Bischoff*

Boy in the oasis, Beni-Abbès, 1948 – Credit: Paul Bowles

'He is wearing a necklace, lots of magic amulets around his neck, a so-called *Baraka*, bringers of luck. That was in Beni-Abbès. I didn't know him, I didn't even talk to him. I just took this photo as I went past... Strange expression.' *Paul Bowles*

Paul Bowles with kif pipe, Cap Spartel (Atlantic Ocean), Tangier, c1969 – Credit: Unknown

Young
acrobats on
the beach,
Tangier, 1956
– Credit:
Paul Bowles

'Everything merely *is*, no questions asked.' *Paul Bowles* ❏

These photographs are taken from Paul Bowles Photographs: 'How could I send a picture into the desert?' *by* **Simon Bischoff** *and* **Paul Bowles**, *(Scalo 1994)*

Support for

INDEX

*I*ndex on Censorship would like to thank the following for their generous contributions to the gala performance of Alan Bennett's *The Lady in the Van:*

Amanda Foreman & Lord Hollick at the after-show party

The Trustees and Directors would like to thank the many individuals and organisations who support *Index on Censorship* and Writers and Scholars Educational Trust, including:

If you would like more information about *Index on Censorship* or would like to support our work, please contact Hugo Grieve, Fundraising Manager on (44) 020 7278 2313 or e-mail hugo@indexoncensorship.org.

FRANK FISHER

Access denied

Last November the UK government announced that 12 million citizens would face strict censorship for the foreseeable future. No one cares, because they're only kids...

In its 1997 UK general election manifesto, the Labour Party pledged to use the Web as an educational tool, establishing a policy to connect schools and colleges to the Internet as soon as possible. Even allowing for the flexibility of pre-election promises, IT enthusiasts were pleased. When in October 1997 the new Labour government announced a final date of 2002 by which all schools, colleges, universities and libraries should be connected via the 'National Grid for Learning', Internet groupies were overjoyed.

But the prospect of every UK child having full Web access was seen as a boon not only by the IT industry and digital utopians. For free expression advocates, this massive expansion of Internet usage was seen as a strong riposte to the growing consolidation and dumbing down of the UK mass media. Our children would be exposed to myriad opinions, countless voices, alternative news angles and news stories. Immersed in a world of diversity and dissent our kids could develop their own values, their own political and moral positions.

Coupled with a commitment from the Department for Education and Employment (DfEE) to cover 'Human Rights' in the updated National Curriculum, including an examination of the value of free speech and tolerance of dissent, it appeared that an appreciation of free expression, warts and all, was close to the government's heart. Sadly, by October 1999, education minister David Blunkett had decided to excise those warts and, in doing so, he initiated one of the largest acts of censorship in British history.

The World Wide Web is a vast, largely unregulated resource – anyone with a halfway decent computer can not only surf the Web, they can also add to it. In consequence, the Internet is not a managed environment. Despite the explosion in mainstream commercial exploitation, the Web remains largely self-published. Websites of favoured dogs and cats jostle with tens of thousands of gurgling infants and excruciating teenage philosophies. Yet pan the datastream deftly enough, and nuggets of creative gold flash up from the unlikeliest places, from the crass but compelling Drudge Report to the macabre pleasures of Dial your Death. Fringe attractions of course, but then it is precisely that fringe which suffers elsewhere as the media focuses on its core commercial content.

Still, it is also true that the media horror stories do have some basis in fact: there are sites on the Web with detailed instructions on bomb-making and improvised firearms, even if the majority draw their deadly information direct from freely available US Army manuals. There are thousands of adult porn sites, even if the commercial pages raise few hackles away from the puritan shores of the UK. There may be some child pornography, even if the National Criminal Intelligence Service recognises that the 'problem' of child porn on the Web is largely illusory. Recent BBC research indicated that fewer than one-hundredth of 1% of sites on the Web were devoted to porn. Compare that with the magazine rack in your local newsagent.

One might have hoped that a government minister would base his decisions on facts not hysteria, aiming for proportionality in his policy making. Not so David Blunkett. In part inspired by, and perhaps in part fearful of, media raving, he has announced that the Web British kids access will not be the World Wide Web at all; in fact our children shall roam the tightly specified streets and heavily monitored avenues of the Whitehall Web – a truncated, narrowed Web, dominated by commercial operations and the neuroses of Nanny Blunkett.

In introducing a package of measures known as the 'Superhighway Safety Pack' Blunkett said: 'I am ... determined to ensure that children are protected from unsuitable material. We all share a responsibility to make sure that children's use of the Internet is appropriate and safe. Suppliers are also expected to offer adequate filtering of the material which can be accessed through their connections to the Internet.' To the student of historical attempts at censorship key words leap out: 'unsuitable', 'appropriate'. To the observer of Internet censorship one word looms frighteningly large: 'filtering'.

The process of connecting schools to the Internet has been largely left to private enterprise. Schools or education authorities have been able to make their own arrangements, or pick from a number of government-approved suppliers. Household names such as Apple, IBM and Bull have been quick to jump into the market, and it is certainly true that the UK education system is now among the most connected in the world. The crucial question is: connected to what?

Following Blunkett's instructions, each supplier is obliged to filter all communications to and from the Internet. Special software is used, either on the desktop or more commonly at server level – ie, at the point of contact to the Internet proper – to monitor student traffic. Certain page requests will be denied, certain downloaded files will be confiscated, certain conversations will be terminated. Even Apple, famed for their 'Think Different' advertising campaign, knuckled under; their National Grid for Learning services page is headed: 'Secure, fast and filtered'. If this software removed all pornography, or information about home-made drugs or firearms, or censored anything else that even anti-censorship campaigners would not want a five-year-old puzzling over and *cut nothing else*, then perhaps we could rest easy. But it does far more.

An example: Bull uses Symantec's I-Gear to filter UK schools access. The software is reckoned to be state of the art: the experience of students in New York suggests otherwise. In autumn 1999, I-Gear began filtering the Board of Education's access. Jan Shakofsky, a humanities teacher at Benjamin Cardozo High School, is reported in the *New York Times* as saying that her students hit the filter whenever they tried to 'research the pros and cons of an issue'. For instance, when looking at gun control they found the National Rifle Association's site was blocked. Similarly, 'Access denied' greeted attempts to research bulimia, child labour, AIDS – even a chapter of John Steinbeck's *Grapes of Wrath* was off limits, because a passage where a starving man suckles at a mother's breast. When it encounters an unfamiliar site, I-Gear uses the tried, if not to be trusted, method of filtering based on a set of prohibited words. However, the software can also check its internal file of blocked sites, regularly updated by Symantec's head office. In fact, left to its default settings I-Gear 'disappears' thousands of websites that find their way on to Symantec's 23 category, hand-compiled list. Who's hand?

Meet Michael Cherry – Michael's a hard-working guy. As systems administrator for Hory County schools, South Carolina, Michael keeps track of every Web page request made by students at local schools, sometimes live, sometimes after the event, perusing print-outs of access requests. His schools use I-Gear, but Michael knows Hory County: 'We're deep in the Bible Belt' he says. He keeps an eye out for any offensive material that slips through the filters, and when he finds such a site, he tells Symantec. Symantec listens, and lists...

Norman Siegel of the New York Civil Liberties Union remarked of I-Gear: 'The blocking program sweeps far too broadly. It significantly undermines teacher's ability to conduct their lessons and students' ability to complete their classroom assignments.'

Back in the UK, another best-selling filter program, CyberPatrol, is the choice of another government-approved supplier, Centerprise. CyberPatrol was one of the first 'censorware' programs, and in the last few years has been found to block the MIT Student Association for Freedom of Expression, Planned Parenthood, the Ontario Centre for Religious Tolerance, the 'Why AOL Sucks' website, the HIV/AIDS Information Center of the Journal of the American Medical Association, the alt.atheism and soc.feminism newsgroups and many more entirely legitimate and non-pornographic sites. This despite CyberPatrol's claims that they evaluate all sites manually. It also has a nasty habit of blocking sites that criticise it or its filtering techniques, or that suggest ways in which students can evade or disable its software.

British astronomer Heather Couper tells the story of a boy complaining to her that he cannot access a website she has co-developed – the filtering software in his school blocks it. Why? Because the site deals with back-garden 'naked eye observations'.

What is clear to anyone with knowledge of filtering software is that any automatic blocking of porn or violence is accompanied by a massive unintentional blocking of innocent and potentially useful sites. In addition, many censorware programs intentionally block non-pornographic dissenting or fringe content in areas such as drug abuse and race issues. Such heavy-handed gagging, if discovered, can only cause harm: does David Blunkett really believe a student will place *more* trust in a teacher's word if all dissenting voices are erased?

Filtering aside, Blunkett's 'Superhighway Safety Pack' also makes clear that material intended for educational purposes has to pass a number of tests before it can be considered suitable for inclusion on the National Grid for Learning website. In fact, the NGfL will not even link to sites unless they abide by strict rules and, again, do not contain 'unsuitable' material. But it doesn't end there. If you want to provide an educational resource online, you not only have to ensure your own site is squeaky clean, you must also ensure that you don't link to any other sites that might contain unsuitable material. Are we still talking pornography? Unfortunately not.

I asked a DfEE spokesman for clarification on exactly what material was considered 'unsuitable' for inclusion on, or linking to, the NGfL site. He was unable to come up with examples so I ran through some of the material *Index on Censorship* currently holds on its website. Linking to mirrors of *Green Anarchist* magazine would not be acceptable – the word 'anarchist' was enough to convince the DfEE that our children would not benefit from reading it. More shocking was the DfEE's reaction to Nadire Mater's ground-breaking article presenting the voices of Turkey's conscript soldiers. Her recording of tales of bullying, drug abuse, murder and atrocity has left Mater facing up to five years' jail for 'defaming the Turkish army' – free speech is not highly regarded in Turkey (*Index* 5/1999). Nor it seems in the UK. British teenagers could not be allowed to read of the brutalising treatment handed out to conscripted Turkish teenagers, nor the mutilations they in turn handed on to Kurds. Why? Perhaps because if they did they might ask why the UK sold arms to Turkey? Perhaps because they might wonder why a NATO army could carry out atrocities against Kurds while bombing others for the same crimes against Kosovars?

It might seem that provocative materials drawing on real-life situations that students see on TV would form a strong basis for classroom discussion, that in Labour's much vaunted 'Citizenship' classes the analysis of democratic values would be enhanced by looking at the limits of tolerance, the boundaries placed on dissent here and abroad.

At times that is the message we hear from government. The reality is very different. Twelve million of our fellow citizens are having to get used to the idea that what they read, what they say, who they talk to is controlled not by their parents or their teachers, but at best by a faceless bureaucrat in Whitehall, at worst by a dull little sub-routine on a UNIX server, humming away in the corner of an anonymous business unit somewhere in our grey unpleasant land. ❏

Frank Fisher

JULIAN PETLEY

Sex and censure

Television is still censured for quantities and quality of sex – but it is perhaps the regulators who have the problem

Sex grabs the attention, and TV schedulers are aware of this. It is the apparently increasing reliance on sex in their programming which has consistently attracted the attentions of the television regulators over the past year – with censure on occasion leading to self-censorship.

Sex was the subject of a special statement in the Broadcasting Standards Commission's *Bulletin* in January 1999. Upholding five complaints against Channel 5's *Compromising Situations*, *Hot Line* and its feature film *Centrefold*, it argued that 'the inclusion, for its own sake, of erotic material in a free-to-air television service is a step change in the use of sex on British television and begins to erode the other difference … between what is available on open access channels and that which is available through pay services. The Commission also considers that their inclusion in a mainstream television service runs the risk of encouraging both the amount of such material and the erosion of standards generally'.

During 1999 programmes against which the BSC upheld, or partially upheld, complaints about sex included *The Bill*, *The Cops*, *Brookside*, *Byker Grove*, *Coronation Street*, *Vice: The Sex Trade*, *Eurotrash*, *Queer as Folk*, Peter Greenaway's film *The Baby of Macon*, *Men Behaving Badly*, *Sex and Shopping*, *A History of Alternative Comedy* and *The Vice*.

When in March 1999 the Independent Television Commission published its *Annual Report 1998,* it criticised C5 for 'the tackiness associated with an increased use of low-budget, erotic drama late in the evening and various factual programmes on sexual themes, including some material that was unacceptable'. *The Real Monty*, *Swindon Superbabes*, *Stags and Hens*, *On the Piste* and *Sex and Shopping* were singled out for criticism as 'overly voyeuristic'. The ITC's *Programme Complaints and Interventions Reports* also reveal that complaints about explicitness in

The Vice, Sex and Shopping and *Vice: the Sex Trade* were upheld.

In terms of the relationship between censure and censorship, it's particularly interesting that the section dealing with *Sex and Shopping* reveals that: 'on being advised of the ITC's concern, the channel had instigated a review of the remaining programmes in the series. Channel 5 subsequently shelved two later programmes ... altogether, as well as carrying out further edits and pixellation ... in line with guidance from the ITC.' The BBC's *Programme Complaints Bulletin* also echoed the BSC in upholding complaints about sexuality in the Christmas edition of *Men Behaving Badly* and *A History of Alternative Comedy*.

The regulators are not concerned solely with sex. Between January and September 1999, the BBC Complaints Unit dealt with 19 complaints under the heading 'sexual conduct' – 2.9% of the total number processed. From January to October, the ITC received 327 complaints relating to 'sexual portrayal' – 9.7% of the total. The most recent figures available for the BSC, from their *Annual Review 1998-99*, show that, in the period covered, 693 complaints concerning sex were received (23% of the total). Of these, 31% were upheld.

But it is the complaints about sex which receive most press attention. Salacious newspaper stories give the impression that there's too much sex on television. But is there? And what do people think about it?

According to a poll commissioned by ITV for the 1999 Edinburgh Television Festival, of the 1,868 people questioned, 64% said that they were happy with the amount of sex on television, provided that sex scenes were not 'tacky or grubby'. Meanwhile, the ITC's *Television: the Public's View 1998* noted that less than a third of viewers had seen or heard anything offensive on television, the lowest proportion since the survey began. The main causes of offence were bad language, followed by violence and then sex.

Meanwhile, the BSC's annual *Monitoring Report* showed that, when asked whether violence, bad language or sex on television caused them most concern, 58% cited violence, 24% bad language and 12% sex. Asked if the amount of sex on television was too much/about right/too little, 38% said 'too much'. This compared with 32% the previous year, but to 41% in 1991, 1992 and 1996 – hardly a rising tide of concern.

The year's most comprehensive surveys of sexuality on television, *Sex and Sensibility* (also from the BSC), similarly found that 36% of respondents, when asked specifically about sex, said that there was too much of it on television. Some 78% of all respondents thought that sexual activity should be depicted if part of a storyline, but 72% felt that sex was being used to increase ratings.

This could itself be seen as a form of censorship. This was made clear by Polly Toynbee's complaint with regard to the BBC's *Adult Lives* that 'serious documentaries are giving way to series like these offering sexy freakshows'. And the role which programmes about sex play in the ratings war was clearly revealed when ITV peremptorily pulled *The Sexual Century* after only two of its five episodes had been aired; clearly, its informative and unexploitative tone was no compensation for lower-than-expected viewing figures (5.2m for the first episode, 3.8m for the second). This also demonstrates that sex is by no means a sure-fire ratings winner. Furthermore, C4's excellent series, *Pornography: the Secret History of Civilisation*, showed that documentaries about sex can be 'serious'.

So, if viewers are aware when, in the words of the organiser of the Edinburgh survey, they are being 'cynically manipulated and led by the genitals', are the regulators being too nannyish and underestimating viewer intelligence when it comes to programmes about sex? Much of the regulators' censure is reserved for inappropriate scheduling rather than for material of which they disapprove per se. However, the BSC still stubbornly insists on upholding complaints from viewers who must only watch certain programmes in order to complain about them (such as C4's *Renegade TV* programmes *Sex Pest* and *Erotica: a Journey into Female Sexuality*, both of which carried strong warnings and were broadcast after 11pm). It also worked itself into a lather over Nick Broomfield's *Fetishes*, accusing him of 'turning the audiences into voyeurs of demeaning and degrading behaviour', apparently unaware that Broomfield's work is precisely *about* movie voyeurism.

Still, such judgments remind us, in the words of C4's deputy director of programmes Karen Brown, that 'our regulatory rules are still tighter than our European neighbours'. We are still not allowed to show penetrative sex on television. Viewers can't see an erect penis on television. Why not? Could the answer be that all these programmes about sex are a symptom not of increasingly liberal attitudes but of our society's deep-seated inability to treat sex in an adult fashion? ❏

Julian Petley is a lecturer in media and communication studies at Brunel University